Tales of the Terminally Awkward

Elizabeth A. Winter-Sharpe

Tales of the Terminally Awkward

Copyright © 2020 Elizabeth A. Winter-Sharpe
All rights reserved.
ISBN: 9798572874273

Elizabeth A. Winter-Sharpe

Dedication

To all those who choose to laugh at themselves and to lift others up. Maybe, just maybe, that's the answer.

And to Jeff.

Contents

ACKNOWLEDGEMENT	7
WELCOME	8
WHIPPERSNAPPER	10
MOM AND THE MAFIA	12
RATCHYPRATCH	15
HOWARD'S END	18
HAPPY TEARS	22
TAG, YOU'RE IT!	26
RULES RULE	29
FAMILY VACATION	30
PET PROJECT	34
THE UNMENTIONABLE INCIDENT	36
ROOKIE	38
MEMORIES OF YOU	43
TIMING IS EVERYTHING	45
QUEEN OF HALLOWEEN	46
RAISING CAIN	48
RING THEM BELLS	51
NO CUTS	54
ALARMED	57
FAWKS PASS	59
LICENSE TO CHILL	62
DRIVE-IN DEBUTANTE	65
ROCK OF AGES	69
CANDY MAN	74
DELIBERATE DATING	78
CROSS MY HEART	81
CAR PARTS	82
STRANGER THINGS	85
DINNER AND A SHOW	88
SAY IT AIN'T SO	91
SIZE DOES MATTER	95
THE "I DO" BLUES	96
A NIGHT AT THE OPERA	98

OUT WITH THE IN-LAWS	102
AN ITALIAN TALE, PRIMA PARTE	105
AN ITALIAN TALE, SECONDA PARTE	110
SPICE OF LIFE	113
PRESCRIPTION FOR TROUBLE	114
BRA-VO	117
INSIDE OUT	121
HEALTHCARE ODYSSEY	124
BACK TO BASICS	127
WHAT'S IN A NAME?	128
THIS LITTLE PIGGY	130
WHAT YOU TALKING ABOUT, WILLIS?	133
GETTING SCHOOLED	136
ODE TO DEAD APPLIANCES	141
QUICKIES	143
DON'T CALL US, WE'LL GO BROKE	150
CONFESSIONS OF A WOULD BE RUM RUNNER	151
MAKING A MEAL OUT OF A SNACK	154
A STRANGE NEW WORLD	157
NO AUTOGRAPHS, PLEASE	159
HIGH MAINTENANCE DÉCOR	162
OPEN DOOR POLICY	163
COMMUNICATION WOES, HANDYMAN HOES	166
FINISHING TOUCH	169
FIFTY SHADES OF WINTER	172
SOCIAL DISTANCING LOG	175
LOOK OUT WORLD	178
JUST A GIGOLO	179
HOW NOW BROWN COW	182
FLYING SOLO	185
MIDWEST GIRLS	188
WISH YOU WERE HERE	191
STAMP OF APPROVAL	194
BE STILL MY HEART	198
RAPPER'S DELIGHT	199
FAN FRENZY	202
PURSE-ONAL FOUL	205
MIXED MARRIAGE	208
THE MOTHBALL INCIDENT	211
ON THE ROCKS	213

SO LONG, FAREWELL	219
ABOUT THE AUTHOR	220

Elizabeth A. Winter-Sharpe

Acknowledgement

If you have one person who is always in your corner, you are lucky. If you have two, you are blessed.

I am incredibly blessed.

Thank you to my dear friend, Kate Tonti, for all your help, support, cheerleading and slightly tough love to bring this book – my dream – to life. You epitomize what it means to be a great friend and I am forever grateful that you are mine.

Thank you to my husband, Jeff Sharpe, for always being by my side and supporting my dreams. I love that we laugh every day. I love that we appreciate each other's strengths and shore up each other's weaknesses. You are everything I could want in a partner, a husband and a friend. I'm forever thankful we found each other. (I still want a goat, though. Or a puppy. Just saying.)

Welcome

When I was about four years old, I came downstairs one December morning to find my parents had put up the Christmas tree. Whether to surprise us or keep decorating mishaps to a minimum, I don't know. *I* was surprised and thought it would be funny to pretend to faint as a result.

Always a safety girl, rather than a pratfall from which I could get hurt, I first sat down on the floor and then sprawled out. Admittedly, it was not quite as effective.

I snuck a peek and noted Mom and Dad just looked at each other and carried on, shaking their heads. For years, I thought they just didn't get me. While true, I later decided they didn't get me because I didn't commit to the comedy. But I had a good reason.

I was born with an awkwardness I never conquered nor was able to manage. After years of trying, I finally learned to laugh about it. Since the alternative was crying, that perspective saved me a bundle on mascara.

It also encouraged me to become a humorist. I've spoken at numerous events, sharing my stories and encouraging people to laugh at their own foibles. Those events always ended with people asking me for a book. (They also end with people confessing their secrets to me. That's a whole other story!)

So, for those who have asked, here it is. This book is a collection of my awkward moments, favorite stories and funny memories. It is my commitment to the comedy in my life.

Elizabeth A. Winter-Sharpe

I have been blessed with extraordinarily funny family and friends, and many of them make an appearance in this book – with my thanks and great affection. I have changed names to protect the innocent (me.) Any errors are my own.

Enjoy.

Whippersnapper

By definition, a whippersnapper is someone who is young, inexperienced and over-confident. I remember an "old" person calling me a whippersnapper. I remember hearing old people using phrases like "Back in my day..." and "There was a time when..." What I don't remember, is joining their ranks. But I realized I've started using those phrases.

As most whippersnappers, I thought I'd always be hip and, if not *cutting* edge, at least *near* the edge. Then one day while reading the obituaries in the local newspaper, I reached for the phone to call my sister because one of our former neighbors had died. Uh-oh. My mother used to call me almost every other day with the "Death Report." My favorite was when Mom called me at work and this conversation ensued:

Mom: Are you busy?
Me: I have a minute. What's up?
Mom: Joe Dokes* died. (*Not his real name.)
Me: Who is Joe Dokes?
Mom: He went to school with your brother.
Me: Mom, he's ten years older than me. I don't know him.
Mom: Well, your brother knows him.
Me: Is he upset about it?
Mom: No, they weren't friends.
Me: Mom, if they weren't friends and I don't know him, why are we talking about it?
Mom: He still died.

Fair point.

Elizabeth A. Winter-Sharpe

Wondering if there were other signs that I'm old, I remember I arrived 40 minutes early for the Grandparent Breakfast last fall at our granddaughters' school.

I recently told someone, "I looked it up on *The* Google."

I can't figure out how to use our plethora of remotes and called my stepson to ask if he knew my Roku password. And what Roku is.

Glum, I stare out the window wondering if socks and sandals are next. Wait a minute. Who is that? Damn it! "Hey, you kids, get off my lawn!"

Mom and the Mafia

My mother was many things – smart, caring, interesting and naïve. Incredibly naïve.

I remember when I was a junior in high school and my mom wanted to have the "Just say 'no' to drugs" talk. After telling me all the dangers of using drugs and the shame I'd bring on the family name if I ever chose to *do* drugs, she summed it up by saying, "I don't ever want to hear about you shooting up marijuana."

Biting my lip to keep from laughing, I solemnly swore I would never do such a thing. "You and Dad raised me better than that, Mom."

Her naiveté' extended beyond drug culture.

We were returning home to Akron from a family vacation, my parents, my sister and her family, and me. I was in my mid-20s.

Always frugal, Mom made reservations at what can only be described as a no-tell motel in nowhere Pennsylvania. It was a motor lodge — the office at the head of a singlewide, one-story building of about 20 rooms, each with the customary parking spot right outside its door. This particular motor lodge was a kaleidoscope of pastel colors from the roof of the carport to the walls of the building and the curtains in the windows. But the door to every room was white.

We arrived about 3:00 in the afternoon. Dad was towing the boat so he pulled into the prescribed spaces on the opposite side of the parking lot. My brother-in-law followed and parked next to him. We checked into our adjoining rooms, which were decked out in textured, orange fleur-de-lis wallpaper, red shag carpet and purple, crushed velveteen bedspreads. My four-year-old niece proclaimed it beautiful.

Dad and my brother-in-law went out to secure the boat. Mom said she was going to clean out the cars. I went to my sister's room to help with the kids.

A few minutes later, we heard a scream, a slamming door and running footsteps. Mom burst through our door, slammed it shut and barred it with her body, arms outstretched. Her face was crimson, her chest, heaving.

"What happened? What's wrong?" my sister and I asked.

"We have to leave," she said, "He's going to kill me."

"Who's going to kill you? What happened?"

"I walked into the wrong room. They all look alike. And I saw him!"

"Him who? What are you talking about?"

"A mafia man. There's a mafia man in one of the rooms. There was a woman, too. I walked in on them."

"Okay, mistakes happen. No big deal."

"Oh, it's a big deal alright. You didn't see what I saw."

Uh-oh. What did she see? A murder in progress? A drug deal? Theft of a kidney? "What'd you see, Mom?"

"He was in bed! With a woman!"

My sister and I looked at each other and tried not to laugh. "Yeah, *and*?"

"They were having S-E-X! On top of the covers! In broad daylight!"

My sister and I dissolved into gales of laughter.

"This is not funny, girls. He's going to come after me. Go get your father. I can't go back out there. We have to call the police and then get out of town."

Before she went on the lam, we tried to calm her down. "It's no big deal, Mom. All the rooms look alike. He doesn't know who you are or which room you're in, not that he'd care anyway. He just forgot to lock the door. Relax."

Then a question came to mind. "Mom, what makes you think he's in the mafia?"

She looked at me as if questioning the validity of my college diploma.

"You mean aside from having S-E-X in the middle of the day?"

"Yeah, Mom, lots of people have sex in the middle of the day, on top of the covers even."

For this comment, I was rewarded with her trademark look: a combination of shock, sadness and utter disappointment.

"Why do you think he's in the mafia?" I asked again.

As if explaining the most obvious thing in the world to someone of dubious intelligence, she replied, "I know he's in the mafia because he was wearing a pinkie ring."

Which made me wonder *not* whether the poor guy was in the mafia, but just how long my mother stood and watched to notice that he was *wearing* a pinkie ring.

Elizabeth A. Winter-Sharpe

Ratchypratch

One of my mom's favorite words was "ratchypratch." If you've never heard it before and are not sure what it means, you're not alone. Near as we can tell it meant something that she considered ridiculous or pointless, occasionally it meant something was incomprehensible. Whatever her definition, "ratchypratch" was bad.

I loved how she related to language. She couldn't find a word that suited her needs, so she made one up.

Words did not evolve in her world, either. Definitions did not change – if they were good enough then, they are good enough now. A case in point -

Many years ago, Mom and I were at a department store and she was buying a sweater. The clerk, who was probably all of 18 years old, said, "This is a pretty sweater."

My mother replied, "Well, my husband shot his wad this morning so I decided I deserved a new sweater."

The clerk turned purple with embarrassment…as did I. I hissed, "Mom! Don't say that!"

She said, "What? I just said your dad shot his wad."

"Don't say it **again**! Do you know what that means?!"

"Yes. I. Do. It means he spent all his money. What do *you* think it means?"

I leaned in to tell her the current meaning of the phrase and I noticed the other shoppers in the area got quiet and leaned in to hear what I had to say.

I whispered it in her ear and she was appalled. At me!

"Elizabeth Ann, how could you say such a thing?! And about your father!"

"I didn't say it! *You* said it!"

"I said no such thing. Why can't you be more like your sister?" Ok, she didn't say that last thing but it was implied.

In addition to her language usage, Mom was also very creative at coming up with explanations for things she didn't understand.

She called me one day and asked me to come by so she could show me some things she bought at a "cute little gift shop" she found.

When I arrived, she was smiling from ear to ear, clearly hiding something behind her back. As soon as I sat down, she whipped that something out from behind her back, yelling, "Ta-Dah!"

With a flourish worthy of a gameshow hostess showing off a Broyhill dinette set, mom showed me her new purchase, which she called a "double vase."

It was blue glass with a round base for the water. It had a tall, thin cylinder on one side and a short, thinner cylinder on the other side.

I couldn't believe my eyes and just stared at my mom as she explained her new double vase, which she placed on the chairside table in the living room. "You see, the tall side is for long-stemmed flowers and the short side is for short-stemmed flowers. It's pretty AND practical!"

I asked, "Mom, what's the name of the cute little gift shop you found?"

"It's a funny name - the Quonset Hut."

Elizabeth A. Winter-Sharpe

Back in the day, the Quonset Hut was what they called a head shop - it sold marijuana paraphernalia, among other things.

I said, "Mom, don't ask me how I know this but what you've got there is called a bong. It's for smoking marijuana."

"It's a double vase."

"No, Mom. Trust me, it's a bong. Do not put flowers in it. And, for goodness sake, take it out of the front window!

Disappointed but undaunted, she brought out her second purchase.

She handed me a little white bag and inside were several small, square, foil-wrapped packages. The foil is camouflage colors and printed on each one is: "Don't let them see you coming." Oh. My. God. She bought camouflage condoms.

My mother was proud and I was curious. Why would she buy these? Could she know what the sentence means? Did she suddenly become hip? I decide to put it to a test.

"Mom, what are these?"

"Well, I don't know for sure but, obviously, they're for hunters. I got them for your father and his hunting buddies."

Nope. Not hip. Just my Mom.

Shaking my head, I said, "Mom, don't give these to anybody. Everybody says they're ratchypratch."

I don't know if I used the word correctly but I hope I made my point.

Howard's End

With all due respect to Michael Jordan and the Hanes people, I invented the "Boxers or Briefs" game. In fairness, I *think* I invented it but I didn't record the moment, so here it is.

It was the late 80's and I was at the courthouse supporting a friend, party to a civil lawsuit. During a break we noticed two attorneys having an intense, whispered conversation.

One of them was about forty-years-old, an inch or so shy of six feet tall, with a lithe runner's build. He had a mop of curly brown hair and when he smiled his warm brown eyes crinkled with humor. And, well, to cut to the chase, he had a very nice rear view, accentuated by well-tailored slacks. It was when he bent to pick up his briefcase that we saw a telltale underwear line.

"He's a briefs man," I whispered to my friend, Mimi. She looked scandalized but giggled, and the game was born.

The other attorney was more difficult to peg. Because he was about sixty, amateurs might automatically call boxers. But something about him gave us pause. He was tall and distinguished, with a full head of salt and pepper hair. He appeared athletic, his broad shoulders and trim waist nicely turned out in a navy Brooks Brothers™ suit. After subtle scrutiny and lengthy discussion, we finally ruled it inconclusive – he could go either way.

We worked our way through the courtroom and out into the hall, categorizing every man we saw. Our game continued at restaurants, stores, sporting events and parties – everywhere we went. Rarely was there a giveaway as with our first unwitting participant so we developed an intricate

Elizabeth A. Winter-Sharpe

set of criteria on which to base our decision including age, athleticism, perceived confidence, clothing style, a rather abstract coolness factor and our gut feeling. Later we'd take it a step further and determine if briefs were colors or tighty whities.

Even though it was a silly game and we never knew the truth about any of the men, we found it fun and felt pretty cocky (no pun intended) about the accuracy of our judgments. But we were always bothered about Howard, the second attorney, the one we deemed inconclusive.

As it happens, Howard and his wife were good friends of my parents.

Howard and Dad were avid sportsmen who took annual hunting and fishing trips together. To my way of thinking, Dad should know the answer we yearned and I need only ask him.

"Dad, Mimi and I were wondering what kind of underwear Howard wears? Boxers or briefs?"

"What?"

"Howard. His underwear. Boxers or briefs? We can't decide and thought you might know."

"What's wrong with you? That's ridiculous. It's none of your business."

"It's just a game, Dad."

"Howard's underwear is a game?"

"No, every man's underwear is a game. We just try to guess whether they wear boxers or briefs."

"Why?"

"It's fun. See, Howard's very athletic and dapper but he's around sixty and when you go hunting he wears that Elmer Fudd hat with the ear flaps."

"Don't you have better ways to spend your time?"

Realizing I wasn't going to get anywhere with Dad, I tried to enlist my mother.

"Mom, aren't you and Dad having dinner with Howard and Katherine this weekend?"

"Yes, we're going to their place."

"Great. I need you to find out what kind of underwear Howard wears – boxers or briefs."

"What?"

"Howard's underwear. Find out if he wears boxers or briefs."

"Even if I would do such a thing, how do you propose I find out?"

"Don't you and Katherine have girl talk?"

"Not about underwear. What kind of talk is that?"

"It's kind of a study, Mom, scientific. Just try to find out, ok?"

"Are you feeling alright?"

"I'm fine. How about this? Excuse yourself to go to the bathroom and accidentally walk into their bedroom. A quick look in their drawers and you'll know, well, about his drawers."

Based on her expression, I hurried on with another option. "You could ask Dad. They hunt together."

Mom just shook her head and walked away, muttering something about all the money they spent sending me to college.

Not one to give up, I called Mom the day after the dinner party. "So, did you find out?"

Sighing heavily, Mom said, "I think he wears camo."

Elizabeth A. Winter-Sharpe

"Camo? Camouflage underwear? Mom, are they boxers or briefs?"

"Oh," she said, "Maybe I mean commando." She laughed and hung up.

All these years later, I still don't know Howard's underwear status. Nor do I know where my mother learned about going commando. I think Mom may have had a game of her own.

Happy Tears

There are four people I'd like to meet before I die: LeBron James, Peyton Manning, President Barack Obama and Michelle Obama.* For the record, I don't give two hoots about sports and can no longer stomach politics. I have long admired all four of them for other reasons. Strangely, as much as I'd like to meet them, I'm scared to meet them.

An old boyfriend used to tell me, "Never meet the people you most admire because they will only disappoint you." I'm just afraid I'll cry the entire time, making the encounter awkward and disappointing for all of us.

I generally don't cry when I'm sad or hurt. I sometimes cry when I'm angry but I *always* cry when I'm really happy or proud of others. If someone says something or does something nice – it doesn't even have to be for me – the tears will flow as if the proverbial floodgates were opened.

I took my eight-year-old granddaughter to her piano lesson. As she plunked out *Old MacDonald*, tears streamed down my face.

I attended my six-year-old granddaughter's Readers' Theater production. She recited her lines: "Q is for Quail. The men hunted for wild quail, turkey, geese, and deer. They caught fish in the rivers." I cried those rivers during her performance.

Some think this is sweet or charming, others find it hilarious, but it causes me great angst. In my family, crying was frowned upon. Basically, if you cried in public, you had better have lost a limb.

Then I shared a special – ironic – evening with my mother. Mom loved the performing arts, particularly singing and dancing. Think Gene Kelly, Ann Miller, Danny Kaye and so on. At some point, she discovered and fell in love with Tommy Tune. She would watch any show or movie in which he appeared. She'd watch any show he choreographed though lament that he wasn't performing.

In the mid-2000's, Tommy was touring with the Manhattan Rhythm Kings and I purchased two tickets for my mom for her birthday. I felt sure she would make an evening of it with her best friend, Joan. Instead, she wanted me to take her.

The show was wonderful. I'd see it again in a heartbeat and would purchase a recording of it today. If I feel like that oh-so-many-years later, imagine how my mother felt that night.

After the show, as we made our way through the huge, three-level theater to the parking deck, we saw that the Manhattan Rhythm Kings had set up a table to sell merchandise. Mom wanted to meet them and buy some CDs so we got in line.

My vantage point allowed me to see the entire lobby, down the three levels of steps to the entrance for the premium seats. To the right of the entrance, I noticed a door and a man standing in front of it, clearly monitoring entry to the room beyond it. I wondered if Tommy was in there meeting patrons and it gave me an idea.

Mom was now chatting animatedly with all the Rhythm Kings so I told her I'd be back in a minute and left her in their care. The man at the door, I think his name was Peter, confirmed that Tommy was in the room with other guests. I asked him if my elderly mother, a HUGE fan of Tommy's, could meet him. Much to my surprise and everlasting gratitude, he said "Yes, of course."

I turned and saw my mother watching me. All I did was crook my finger and she knew. Somehow, she knew her moment had arrived and my 77-year-old, arthritic, asthmatic mother summoned her inner Flo-Jo.

Tales of the Terminally Awkward

She took off across the upper lobby, dodging groups of other theatergoers who had gathered to talk, spinning around lollygaggers who stepped in her path, hurdling a dropped hat and leaping two steps at a time down the three levels to where Peter and I were waiting.

Peter took us into the private room and there he was – 6' 6½", handsome, smiling, laughing, Tommy Tune. He walked over and Peter introduced us, noting that my mother was a huge fan. Tommy took her hand and thanked her for coming to the show *and* for being so kind as to take the time to meet him. My mother simply burst into tears.

For the next two uncomfortable minutes, my mother cry-talked to Tommy about how much she loved him. He looked at me in alarm and I just shrugged my shoulders and mouthed, "She's okay." (I was a little teary myself because they were so kind.)

Tommy autographed her playbill, thanked her again, and wished her well. Peter and I both made motion to escort her to the door. Just like that, the tears stopped and my mother coyly said, "So, Tommy, where are you staying tonight?"

Three mouths collectively dropped open – Tommy, Peter and me. Tommy looked at Peter and hesitantly said, "I'm not really sure..." trailing off. To which my mother responded, "You're more than welcome to stay at my house. I'll even make you breakfast."

"Oh. Thank you. But, umm. We'll be fine," he said haltingly.

"I think you'll be more comfortable at my place." she sing-songed.

I jumped in, "Mom, the hotel will charge him if he cancels now," thinking it would appeal to her depression-era sensibilities, no matter how wealthy he may be.

"How about breakfast?"

"He can't, Mom. They have to hit the road very early in the morning to get to their next show. We'd better go."

Thanking them both again, I hustled Mom out of there.

I don't know if she was being s*eriously* friendly or flirting with him. Still, <sniff> they were so kind to my mother. <sniff> So nice. <SNIFF> Does anyone have a tissue?

*I've written Michelle Obama four times over 18 months to ask for a letter of congratulations for my stepdaughter (a huge fan) for earning her *second* Master's degree in education and devoting her life to education, specifically, middle-school students. Such a request is an option on Mrs. Obama's website. Four times. Eighteen months. Nada. Bubkes. I still want to meet her but I'm a little mad. I'd probably still cry.

Tag, You're It!

My mother was a beautiful woman. People often commented that she looked like Elizabeth Taylor. I could never imagine my mom as flirtatious or coquettish so I think their similarities ended with their features.

From the stories Mom told me about her dating years, I always thought she seemed flustered when it came to men. However, when it came to her courtship with my Dad, Mom would smile and say, "Your dad chased me until I caught him."

As a child, I believed this to be a strange, elaborate game of tag in which the pursued suddenly and unexpectedly turns around and grabs the pursuer in a bear hug. Then they had to get married. My belief was reinforced every time I overheard a comment about a girl who "had to get married." I would shake my head knowingly and mutter, "Tag, you're it."

Though Mom and Dad had lucked out in this game of matrimony tag, I thought it was a pretty frivolous and risky way for a woman to get a husband. Naïve, even. So when it came to matters of men, right or wrong, I always thought of my mom as naïve.

A year or so after Dad died, Mom received an email from Donald, a high school classmate. He was planning their 55th high school reunion, had tracked her down online and was hoping she would attend the shindig.

They exchanged a few emails and Mom finally agreed to go to the reunion, which was in upstate New York, where they had gone to high school.

Elizabeth A. Winter-Sharpe

We didn't want her to drive by herself. A family friend, also from upstate New York and now living near us, arranged to visit friends in the area that same weekend and kindly took Mom with her.

Mom stayed with our cousins who dropped her off at the Ramada Inn for the reunion. When she was ready to leave, she was to call them and they would pick her up. All in all, a well-crafted plan for a septuagenarian good time.

About 8 o'clock that evening I was surprised to see my Mom calling me. "Hi Mom. Did you have fun at the reunion?"

She answered in her trademark stage whisper. "Yes. I'm still here. I don't know what to do. Don invited me back to his room for a drink. Should I go? What if he gets ideas? What if people talk? What about my reputation?"

Never in a million years did I think I'd be having this conversation with my mother. But what can you do? Girl power.

I started with the easy stuff. "Mom, your decisions are no one's business but yours. Plus, they all live hundreds of miles from you. Don't worry about what others say about you and certainly not about your reputation. You're a wonderful person. What's important is, do you *want* to go to his room?"

"Well, I don't know. It might be nice to talk with him for a while. Our French teacher is here and you can't get a word in edgewise with her around!"

(For the record, the French teacher's first job out of college was at Mom's high school so she was just a few years older than this group of students.)

"OK, so if you want to hang out with him, the only other thing to ask yourself is, do you feel safe with him? And, I guess, um, just in case, um…do you have protection?"

"Protection? You know I don't like guns!"

Guns.

"On second thought, Mom, maybe it's time you called it a night."

Elizabeth A. Winter-Sharpe

Rules Rule

A favorite story of my dad's:

He went on an annual hunting trip with a group of friends. They had two rules: 1) Each person had one day on which he cooked for the entire group and 2) The first person who complained about another's cooking had to cook for the rest of the week.

On their way to the remote Pennsylvania town where they were to hunt, car trouble delayed them so that they didn't arrive until well after the town's only grocery store had closed. They went on to the cabin, planning to return in the morning for groceries.

The first up in the morning, Dad poked through the kitchen cupboards, and, to his delight, found some flour, sugar and a few other odds and ends. Although he had never made pancakes, he thought surely he had discovered most of the important ingredients.

Just as the first pancake was done, he turned to find one of the guys standing behind him, plate in hand. No sooner had he served him than the others came in and got in line.

As he was serving the rest, the first jumped up and yelled, "These pancakes taste like shit!"

Silently, they all turned to look at him, and, remembering the rule, he quickly added, "Which is just the way I like them."

Family Vacation

I was fortunate to be born into a family that valued travel. My parents thought an annual family vacation was important and it laid a foundation for lifelong wanderlust. Most of the time we went to the Outer Banks, but we did visit other places on occasion.

When I was 12, my parents took my sister and me to Florida for a week. Our first stop was a surprise for me – a visit to Disney World. I had my picture taken with Snow White, which must have bothered Grumpy because he followed me around the park all day and would stomp his foot at me whenever I noticed him. The only downside was getting stuck on the "It's a Small World" ride. Forty-five minutes of that song is painful.

After Disney World, we rented a houseboat and spent the rest of the time living on the St. Johns River. I'm sure it was Dad's idea. He loved being on the water, whereas my mother liked being next to it. Poolside. With a good book. And a beverage.

Most days on the river ended with Dad maneuvering the boat as close to shore as he could so Mom could jump from the boat and tie it to a tree. It never went well and Mom slid into the water more than once.

One night we docked at a small island inhabited only by a ranger and his wife. I think it was unusual for them to see other adults, so they invited my parents over for dinner.

Elizabeth A. Winter-Sharpe

My sister and I stayed on the boat, playing cards and otherwise entertaining ourselves. Later, I was brushing my teeth before bed and as I bent down to spit into the sink, I saw a pair of eyes looking up at me. I shrieked and my sister came running only to shriek with me when the owner of the eyes – a bright green frog with toothpaste on his head - jumped up through the pipe and into the tiny bathroom.

We stumbled out of the bathroom and ran to the galley, screaming the entire time. Ultimately, we summoned our inner courage, caught the frog and released it back into the water.

The worst part was realizing all sorts of creatures could come calling, and not just through the sink. I said many prayers using that bathroom.

My first experience traveling without my parents was when I was 15 and my 23-year-old sister took me to Clearwater Beach, Florida, for spring break. It was a kind and generous thing for her to do and we had a blast. I always looked older than my years, which ensured I had a few questionable experiences. No worries though, as any questionable experience came to a screeching halt as soon as I opened my mouth.

We hung out with a family friend and his buddy, and one evening they took us to a little neighborhood bar. Try as I might to "be cool" and have a glass of bad wine, I was nervous, expecting the police to swoop in at any moment and arrest me.

I relaxed when I saw a message written on a chalkboard behind the bar that said, "Age is a matter of the mind. If you don't mind, it doesn't matter." I believed this to be the philosophy, the *rule*, of the bar, meaning it was okay for me to drink alcohol while there.

I made quite an impression on the bartender when I made a point to tell him, "I just want to assure you that I do *not* mind being under age." I was yanked out of there so fast I'm pretty sure my words were still hanging in the air.

Tales of the Terminally Awkward

Enamored with Clearwater Beach, I returned for spring break when I was 20, this time with a college friend. At that time, the drinking age in Florida was 19; Ohio's was 21. We seized the opportunity and stocked up at the liquor store before we even checked into our hotel. The next day, we invited some new friends to our room for drinks before we all went out.

We were gussied up and feeling quite worldly, waiting to entertain our new friends. Shortly before the appointed hour, there was a knock on the door. I flung it open with a "Woo-hoo! Let's party!" only to see my parents standing in the doorway. I think my heart may have stopped for a moment.

My parents were pretty cool about the whole thing. Mom clearly disapproved but had made her point – she could show up anywhere, anytime. Dad shrugged his shoulders – I was legal in Florida. He was pleased we had Scotch.

As for our expected guests, my friend slipped out to give them a heads up in case they didn't want to hang with my parents. They did not.

It also cured me of any desire to drink – something I do rarely even now.

By far, our favorite family vacation spot was the Outer Banks.

Once, in my mid-twenties, Dad and I were fishing in a little inlet in the Pamlico Sound and the Ocracoke ferry was approaching. Dad reeled in but told me to keep my line in the water to troll as he moved our boat.

I'm not good at estimating distance, but we could clearly see people on the shore though their faces were indistinct. As dad moved the boat, I noticed a tug on my line. At the same time, I noticed a man on the beach wave to me. I was flattered, thinking my red and white striped tube top, sun-kissed skin and newly permed hair had all worked together to get me noticed, even from afar. I giggled and waved back, then turned my attention to my line as the tugging became stronger.

Elizabeth A. Winter-Sharpe

Dad began to pull away and the man's waving became more animated. I waved again. My inner monologue declared I needed to buy more tube tops.

Dad then told me to keep reeling to bring in the fish but be careful as he was going to have to go more quickly than he anticipated, to avoid the worst of the wake.

As I reeled in my line, the man's waving became frantic and he began jogging down the beach in the same direction we were headed. "Wow," I thought, "He's got it bad for me!"

Just as my hook cleared the water, I noticed it was *not* a fish on my line but, inexplicably, another hook, connected to another fishing line, connected to a pole, which was held by a man now running down the beach and with his middle finger extended in the air. I disengaged our hooks and gave him one final wave, choosing to ignore the one-finger salute.

Dad thought the entire scene was hilarious. Arriving back at the cottage that afternoon, Dad announced, "Beth caught a man today!" Mom's response was simply, "Finally!" She sighed heavily, but was not surprised, when she heard I let him get away.

Pet Project

Some say that pets and their owners begin to look alike. In my case, my dog began to act like me. More specifically, he got himself into awkward or embarrassing situations but was plucky enough to rise above it.

Mitch started out as my parents' dog. Dad was an avid hunter and Mitch was a German Shorthaired Pointer. If you're not familiar with the breed, they're known for their ability to sniff out, then literally point their leg in the direction of the prey.

Mitch went to obedience school and had extra training in hunting – graduating first in his class. Ultimately, I think he demonstrated the difference between theory and practice.

The first time Dad took Mitch hunting, he got him out of the car, told him to sit and then went to the back gate to get his gear. When he turned back, Mitch had gotten back in the car. It was cold out, thank you very much. It happened twice more before Dad realized Mitch was hearing what Dad said but considered them suggestions rather than commands.

Mitch did point out a duck that morning, Dad made the shot and it landed in a pond. Dad shouted, "Mitch! Fetch!" And Mitch looked at him as if to say, "Who? ME?" Mitch refused to go near the duck or the water and Dad had to retrieve the duck himself.

Over time, it became evident that Mitch was scared of ducks. Somehow, he seemed to understand his role as an aide to the family provider, though, and on one of his very few hunting trips, Mitch jumped a fence into a cow pasture and tried to catch a cow. He was unsuccessful but you have to admire the effort.

Elizabeth A. Winter-Sharpe

Shortly thereafter, Mitch came to live with me. He was a smart dog until he wasn't. For example, if you asked him if he wanted to have a sleepover with Grandma and Grandpa, he would pick up his food bowl, run outside and jump into the backseat of the car. When in the car, he knew by the turn I took if we were going to the vet (he'd start to whine) or to visit my parents.

On the other hand, my roommate put him in the basement one day while we were both at work. It was a very nice basement, by the way: large, temperature-controlled, with a rug and a sofa he could sleep on, a bowl of water and his toys. Apparently objecting to a closed door leading to the rest of the house, Mitch decided to chew his way out of the basement. Unfortunately, he started at the *bottom* of the banister so he didn't get very far. Then again, that was his last day in the basement so maybe he was smart.

In addition to ducks, Mitch was also scared of the vet. In the waiting room, all 65 pounds of him would crawl onto my lap. He'd put his front paws over my shoulders, bury his head in my neck and whine.

Unfortunately, we went to the vet regularly to get Mitch's nails clipped. I tried to do it once and the first nail I clipped bled. It was awful. To save the rug and the furniture, I decided to wrap his paw in a maxi pad and put a sock over it. Ingenious!

Mitch didn't seem to object so I put him outside on his run. A short while later, I heard some laughter. Investigating, I found several of my neighbors standing around pointing at Mitch. He had managed to get the sock off his paw and the maxi pad's adhesive tape off the pad, so he was now wearing the maxi pad like a mustache.

He was probably just going for the joke. Yep, that's my dog.

The Unmentionable Incident

I do not have children. Strangely, though, I haven't escaped some of those embarrassing moments that come with children, the ones that usually involve them sharing highly personal information with the world.

It was mid-November and the whole family – siblings, spouses, niece and nephews – was at my parents' home for the weekly Sunday dinner. Everyone was in the great room talking and I went to the other room to get something from my purse.

My sister-in-law followed me and said, "I hear you and your mom went shopping yesterday."

"Yes."

"I hear you bought underwear."

"Yes." (Why Mom felt this was newsworthy, I'll never know.)

In an effort to be funny, she asked, "Crotchless underwear?"

Never one to let an opportunity pass, I jokingly replied, "Of course, you know that's the only kind I wear!"

From behind us came a tiny voice, belonging to our six-year-old niece, who asked, "What's crotchless underwear?"

As I stood speechless, mouth agape, my quick-thinking sister-in-law said, "They're underwear for poor people." (Because they use less fabric, you see . . .)

My niece accepted this answer without comment and ran off to play. Whew! Crisis averted!

The next evening my sister called me. "Guess where I just came from?" she asked. "No idea," I replied. "The principal's office," she said, which, by the way, was in a Catholic school.

I settled in to hear what happened.

"They're having a canned food drive at school. The teacher told the class that they need to help poor people and asked them each to bring in a can of food or money to give to the poor."

"That's nice," I said, "But why did you have to go to the principal's office?" (I started to feel a little uncomfortable but couldn't put my finger on why.)

"Well y*our* niece raised her hand and asked if they could give food to her Aunt Beth because her Aunt Beth is poor. Do you know *why* she thinks her Aunt Beth is poor? No? The teacher didn't either. So she asked why she thought her Aunt Beth was poor and your niece said – in front of God and everybody – 'because she wears crotchless underwear.' I've never been so embarrassed!"

Me either.

Yes, I was sorry for the poor teacher who then had to deal with an entire class of 6-year-olds who'd learned a fun new phrase, and no doubt introduced it to their extended family at Thanksgiving dinner.

But then again, I had my own problems. Eventually those kids learned a new word or moved on to 2nd grade. For me, in an effort to "save my reputation," my mom promised to make a point of telling everyone we knew, "My daughter, Beth, does NOT wear crotchless underwear."

<Sigh>

Rookie

I wanted to be an aunt since I was 10 years old. I nagged my siblings, particularly my sister, endlessly about getting married and having a baby.

Imagine arriving home from a date and your little sister asking you, "Do you think you'll marry him? Does he want kids?"

I was 20 when my niece was born and 24 when my nephews were born. It was the best! I used to take them to the park or restaurants and we would have sleepovers at my house. I remember one summer day when I took them on a jaunt and we sang Christmas carols in the car. They thought I was wild because I sang a Christmas song in July, but those were the only songs I knew all the words to. Sometimes I'd make up new words. My niece still giggles when she thinks about my version of *Home on the Range*... "and we can eat candy all day!"

I was always surprised when my siblings expressed frustration with any of the kids. Near as I could tell, they were delightful.

One fall, my sister asked if I'd take care of my niece and nephew for a long weekend while she and the hubs went out of town. I was thrilled! They were eight and four, so pretty self-sufficient. How hard could it be? We would have so much fun!

I picked up the kids from my parent's house on Thursday after work. Grandma had fed them and their homework was done so I only had bath time and bedtime.

Elizabeth A. Winter-Sharpe

In the morning, they had to go to school and I had to go to work so my plan was to make breakfast while they were washing and dressing. While they were eating breakfast, I would get ready.

Rookie mistake #1: Believing children will actually do what you tell them to do, when you tell them to do it.

I woke them up and instructed them to wash, dress, and come downstairs for breakfast. When they didn't appear for breakfast, I went to investigate. Neither had washed or dressed.

My nephew was under his bed playing with his cars. My niece was making a potholder with one of those plastic toy looms. So, I had to get them ready and downstairs for breakfast, leaving me just minutes to get dressed because we were now running terribly late.

Normally, my niece would walk around the corner and wait at the bus stop with other neighborhood kids. I really preferred to take her to school – nothing would happen on my watch - but I learned that if a child normally rides the bus and you take her to school instead, you will "ruin her life." I then offered to wait at the bus stop with her and I learned that would "embarrass her to death." So we compromised, meaning she did her usual, and I didn't tell her but drove the car slowly behind her and waited until she got on the bus, ultimately looking exactly like the very kidnapper I feared.

In the meantime, my nephew decided he was not going to preschool but going to work with me instead. No amount of reasoning worked so I finally told him it was illegal for aunties to take nieces or nephews to work and he'd have to take it up with the governor.

The people at his preschool weren't particularly friendly. They kept giving me strange, somewhat alarmed, looks. I assumed it was because I was dropping off a child who was screaming, "I WANT TO TALK TO THE GOVERNOR!"

By the time I got to work, I was 40 minutes late. I ran in, out of breath, and my colleagues took one look at me and said, "What happened to you? Do you need help?"

Tales of the Terminally Awkward

"Oh, I just had the kids this morning. Nothing I can't handle."

To which one said, "Really? You're wearing two different shoes!"

I looked down and sure enough, I was wearing one black pump and one blue flat. I retreated to the restroom and looked in the mirror. Oh, my God! I had bed hair, no makeup and my clothes didn't match each other or my shoes! How do parents do this?

We had McDonald's for dinner and watched a movie before bedtime. I was exhausted and grateful that the next day was Saturday.

Rookie mistake #2: I asked them what they'd like for breakfast.

One said an omelet and one said pancakes. Since I asked, I figured it was only fair to make both.

Presenting pancakes to my nephew, he said, "I don't like pancakes."

"Then why did you ask for them?"

"I forgot. It's French toast that I like."

Sighing inwardly, I threw the pancakes away and made French toast.

Serving the French toast, he said, "Oh, that's right. It's French Toast I don't like. It's pancakes I like."

I tried to convince him that they're virtually the same thing but it didn't work and I had to start all over. Being the cool Aunt is hard work!

After breakfast, I sent them to wash, dress and do their chores while I cleaned up the kitchen. I had no idea how many crises a kid has in an average morning but my niece couldn't find her favorite head band, my nephew managed to create havoc with a glue stick he found somewhere, the dog stole someone's socks and so on. By the time they got dressed and breakfast was cleaned up, it was time for lunch. I was still in my pajamas.

Rookie mistake #2, reprise: I asked what they wanted for lunch. One voted for McDonald's, the other wanted pizza. We compromised on grilled cheese and a hot dog.

Rookie mistake #3: By the time lunch was over and I had cleaned up, it was about 2:30. I was still in my pajamas. I told the kids I was going to take a shower and they were not to do anything for 15 minutes.

I was in the shower, wondering how I was going to make it through the next two days, turned and saw my darlings in the bathroom along with five of their closest friends.

Luckily, the glass was frosted so it wasn't an X-rated show but I hadn't bargained for this. I stuck my head out and said, "What are you doing in here and who are all these kids?" Well, their parents should be proud because they introduced each child by name and with an interesting conversational tidbit: "This is Joey; he lives next door. This is Brittany; she has a puppy. This is Michael; he has a baby brother." And so on.

"Thanks. Very nice. What do you want?"

"Can we have a popsicle?"

At this point, I was thinking they could have cigarettes and beer but didn't say it. I sent the kids home, telling them it's illegal for aunties to give sweets to children who are not related to them. They learned a lot about the law that weekend.

Dinnertime arrived and I told them I was making spaghetti. A chorus of complaints erupted because they both had other ideas. Then, without thinking, from somewhere deep inside of me, this came out: "This is not a restaurant. You eat what I put in front of you or you will go hungry."

It happened. It took less than 48 hours, but I became my mother.

Tales of the Terminally Awkward

The last night, I tucked my niece into bed and she told me I was "the coolest Aunt ever." Tucking in my nephew, when I kissed him goodnight he grabbed my face and said, "Auntie Beth, you took care of us *good*."

Overall, it was a great weekend but I had to wonder: I'm college-educated, manage my own home, and direct a multi-million dollar department at work. How could taking care of two well-behaved, self-sufficient kids for four days exhaust me, mentally and physically?

With great respect to parents everywhere, I decided being an auntie is my sweet spot.

Update: Being a grandma is the BOMB!

Elizabeth A. Winter-Sharpe

Memories of You

After our parents died, my siblings and I were cleaning out their home and found a wooden table leg that did not match any table they'd ever had. I wondered where they got *just* a table leg and why. It was a silly thing but it reminded me of a question I had addressed a few years earlier: If you should die unexpectedly, would your survivors find anything embarrassing in your home?

My (now) ex-husband and I had just moved into a new home and invited my entire family over to celebrate birthdays. My sister, always thoughtful, brought me a housewarming gift. I was touched.

As others opened birthday gifts, I pulled my gift from its gift bag. Inexplicably, it was a "personal pleasure device," 12-inches long and neon purple. Shocked, I shoved it back into the bag and stuffed the bag under my chair.

My mother, ever naïve, exclaimed, "That looked pretty. Is it a new spatula? Pass it around so everyone can see it."

My sister was laughing hysterically. Ex demanded to know what I said to my sister that would prompt such a gift. To which my mom responded, "Every good cook can use another spatula!" (Hmmm, naïve and yet wise.)

I finally convinced Ex it was just my sister's sense of humor but I had another problem. What if I died unexpectedly and someone found it? I'd be mortified! Yes, I know I'd be dead. Still - I had to get rid of it! But how?

It was not as simple as putting it in our trash. Trash cans in our neighborhood were regularly knocked over and with my luck "it" would tumble into our driveway for all the neighbors to see.

Tales of the Terminally Awkward

I certainly couldn't take it to work or a public trash container to throw it away. What if I was in an accident while on the way? The fact that you're wearing clean underwear will go unnoticed in the emergency room if you're carting around a purple personal pleasure device.

I cleverly decided to put it in the trash can of our elderly neighbors who lived across the street. On trash pickup night, I waited in my darkened home, watching for signs that the neighborhood was asleep. About 2 a.m. I crept out of the house, careful not to wake Ex who was unaware of my plan.

Thinking it would be quieter, I chose not to wear shoes, which made crossing the gravel-strewn street painstaking and painful. Intent on where I was walking, I paid no attention to where I was going and walked straight into the neighbor's trash container, knocking it over and tumbling over top of it. The contraband flew out of my hand and together we set off their motion detector, flooding the driveway with light.

As I scrambled to right the trash can I was horrified to discover my sister had given me the deluxe model because it both vibrated and lit up. A purple beacon in their side yard, it was pointing at me and humming an ode to my guilt. I threw myself on top of it and scuttled to the bushes beside my neighbors' garage. Frantically trying to simultaneously hide the purple neon light and turn it off, I looked like a hyperactive baton-twirler.

My neighbors were either undisturbed or unconcerned and a short while later I was again in relative darkness. I crept to their trash can, quietly lifted the lid and disposed of my gift.

I returned home, heart pounding, relieved I had accomplished my mission with no one being the wiser. I slipped into bed, closed my eyes and heard Ex say, "Nice light saber, Luke Skywalker."

I knew I'd end up embarrassed.

Elizabeth A. Winter-Sharpe

Timing Is Everything

For a time, I attended a large, beautiful Catholic church. I liked the priests, particularly the elder priest as his sermons were interesting, thought-provoking and considerate of other viewpoints.

One Sunday morning, the elder priest noted that most parishioners did not know the stories represented by the stained glass windows that lined the back of the church and that would be the day we would learn about them.

He asked us to stand, turn and face the back of the church. At that exact moment, a latecomer opened the door to enter the church only to see the entire congregation turning around, seemingly to witness his late entrance.

The latecomer's mouth fell open and his face turned red. The parishioners were silent. Slowly, the latecomer backed out and closed the door. Realizing how it must have looked and felt, everyone burst into laughter.

I don't know if that poor man ever came back to church but, if he did, I'd bet he was on time.

Queen of Halloween

A month or so into first grade, I became excited about Halloween because our school celebration would include a costume contest. I couldn't imagine any outcome other than my winning because I had decided to be an Arabian princess. I don't know where I got the idea but it was my heart's desire.

In my memory, I had only worn a packaged costume straight from the drug store holiday aisle but an Arabian princess costume would not be found there. In a flash of frugal ingenuity, my mother removed the white lace curtains from the windows of the bedroom I shared with my sister. She wrapped one curtain around my body, looped a corner over each shoulder, and fastened it with a safety pin. She took another curtain and wrapped it around my head, covering my face other than my eyes, and fastened it with a safety pin, too.

She proclaimed me finished, which I interpreted to mean I was the most beautiful Arabian princess ever.

Mom had left the costume pinned to make it easier to put on at school but I couldn't make heads nor tails of it. I finally shimmied into one curtain but could only find one armhole. I yanked the other curtain over my head, careful to leave only my eyes showing. Despite these difficulties, in my mind the transformation was complete.

We paraded through the halls for the upper classmen and walked around the block so the school's neighbors could see us. I magnanimously waved to everyone, certain they were in awe at the sight of me.

Elizabeth A. Winter-Sharpe

We then marched into the social hall where the priest was to announce the winner of the best boy costume and the best (most beautiful!) girl costume. I made sure to stand near the front so I could more easily collect the $2 prize.

The priest quieted the room to announce the winners: the boy dressed like Daniel Boone and . . . *not me* but a girl dressed like a pilgrim! He lifted her up so the entire room could admire her. Even at six years old I noted it was a very nice pilgrim costume, decidedly *not* from the holiday aisle at the drug store. Still, I was an *Arabian princess* and he had barely glanced at me. Could it be that I *was not* the most beautiful Arabian princess ever?

I was a good sport and clapped for the winners but at that moment, I began to doubt my own judgment about myself, and seriously question that of my mother, not to mention the priest.

Looking back, I realize I was a hot mess that looked exactly like a little kid in a Catholic uniform with lace curtains haphazardly wrapped around her, completely un-princess-like. My only regret is that there's no photographic evidence to vindicate one of us.

Raising Cain

I was raised Catholic. My family wasn't uber-Catholic but my parents saw to it that we went to church once a week, received the sacraments, and there was at least one rosary, a children's Bible, and some prayer cards in the house, so we had the basics.

I find matters of faith interesting, particularly when it comes to children. Consider my siblings. Without reservation, they would question things they didn't understand and challenge those things they disagreed with.

In contrast, I was a "go along to get along" child. If I had a question, I would first try to come up with an explanation on my own. Failing that, I would carefully choose the person, time and place to ask. Most of the time, I'd just figure the adults knew what they were talking about and leave it at that.

As did my siblings, I went to Catholic school. Overall, it was fine but I had mixed feelings about religion class. Jesus seemed nice, as did Mary, and most of the disciples. But there were so many horrible, cruel people!

And what is this about the Garden of Eden being all Eve's fault? Adam had no responsibility for actually taking a bite of the apple? It seemed so wrong, but I prudently kept it to myself.

There were a couple of other bumps in first grade. First, one day we were all supposed to bring a boxed lunch wrapped like a present that we would trade with a classmate. I don't know why we were doing it nor do I know why my mother refused to allow me to participate.

My teacher sent me to the principal's office with my paper-bagged lunch. The principal put my sandwich, apple and two Hydrox cookies in a box, added a rosary so I could pray for my mother, and wrapped it up. I was told to return to my class and just keep my lunch, unwrapping it when all the other kids did.

On one hand, it was nice of the principal to help me be part of the activity. On the other hand, she put me in the position of disobeying my mother. Who was the higher power here? I didn't know, but felt guilty and hid the rosary when I got home. I did pray for my mother though, just in case.

The second bump was as traditional to Catholics as bingo night – the selling of religious-themed candles and wrapping paper. My mother had me take the sales sheet back to the principal and tell her, "My parents are not raising me to be a salesman!" I guess mom took a little power back.

The year ended and we moved on to second grade, which is a big year for Catholic children. They make their first communion, but before that they must make their first confession. It was a pivotal event in my life. Why?

I lied at my first confession. There, I said it. What a relief.

To prepare for this important occasion, we learned we're all sinners, *born* with original sin for something we didn't even do. That did not sit well with me. As most kids, I felt I was blamed for plenty of things I didn't do and bristled at the unfairness.

We learned about mortal sins, which *I* understood to be killing someone or being "too nice" to your neighbor's spouse. (Wait. What about "love thy neighbor?" And which person was the neighbor and which person was the spouse?) Venial sins were any other wrongdoing, or so I believed.

We learned the practice of confessing, which was going into a dark closet where only God could see your shame, reciting your sins and the Act of Contrition, and receiving your penance.

Tales of the Terminally Awkward

We were in for a surprise though! This year we were not confessing in the dark closet. This year, we were going to meet with the priest and confess our sins right to his face!

I was far less worried about the venue than what I would actually say. Mortal sins were out. I hadn't killed anyone and had successfully avoided the neighbors for the previous two months so I couldn't be accused of being too nice to any of them. That left the venial sins, which were pretty vague.

I was a good kid; my parents didn't put up with much. Still, I knew better than to tell the priest I hadn't sinned because only Jesus was without sin. But weren't we supposed to try to be like Jesus? It was all so confusing.

I was thinking about all this while we waited in the church for our turn. Finally, I was beckoned into the sacristy. I noted the priest was seated in a large ornate chair and was wearing his vestments and a purple stole. This *was* an occasion.

Sitting in the metal folding chair across from the priest, I got through the initial rituals easily enough. Then, feeling like I'd better make it worth his while, I started making up sins: I did not make my bed, I argued with my sister and I didn't do a homework assignment. None were true – so far as I could remember – but all were plausible. Boom! Sinner.

The priest told me to behave myself, and my penance was to say five Our Fathers and ten Hail Marys. I was forgiven for sins I didn't commit and no one was the wiser. Except for me, thanks to the guilt that has been my constant companion ever since.

I still avoid the neighbors, too. Those mortal sins are bad news!

Elizabeth A. Winter-Sharpe

Ring Them Bells

Being Catholic, my family went to mass once a week and my siblings and I went to Catholic school. Mostly.

When I was very young, my mom made sure we sat in the front during Mass, thinking that all the activity would keep me attentive. What I remember is the bells.

Next to the altar was a set of shiny gold altar bells. Three times during the mass, the altar boy would twist the handle so the bells chimed. It was the most beautiful sound I'd ever heard and I loved seeing them flash in the light. My earliest church memory is longing to, with apologies to Liza Minnelli, "ring them bells." For Jesus. Yes, some for me, but mainly for Jesus.

In the spring of my 3rd grade year, the priest stopped in our classroom with a special announcement: It was time to sign up if you wanted to be an altar boy.

My hand shot up instantly. My time had come – I could almost feel my hand on those bells. I was not at all concerned by the vernacular. True, all the altar boys were, indeed, boys, but probably because no girls had applied.

"No, Bethie. This is only for boys," the priest said.

"Why?"

"Because they're altar *boys*."

"Why can't there be altar *girls*?" I looked around for support from my sister classmates but there was none.

"Because girls aren't allowed on the altar."

Tales of the Terminally Awkward

"What?"

"Well, unless they're cleaning it."

"WHAT?"

I knew better than to argue with a priest so I took it to the highest local authority I knew – my parents. I guess they thought nine was too young to know about sexism and patriarchy. Instead, I learned that life isn't fair and it sucked to be me.

Still, I wondered why anyone, especially people of faith, would think it okay to treat girls unfairly. Clearly, I wasn't that well read yet. Reluctantly, I accepted the situation and life returned to normal.

Shortly thereafter, 3rd graders from across the city went to a ballet. It was nice but there were students from another school seated behind us who were a bit disruptive.

Later that day as we filed outside for recess, the principal stopped me and asked about the ballet.

"It was really nice," I told her. "We had fun."

"Did everyone behave," she asked.

"We did, but the kids behind us were bad."

Lining up after recess to return to the classroom, a classmate confronted me. "I heard you tell the principal we were bad at the ballet."

"No, I didn't."

"Yes, you did. You're stupid!"

And just like that, I'd had enough. This was not how you were supposed to treat other people. I walked out the school door and walked the one mile home.

Elizabeth A. Winter-Sharpe

No one was home when I arrived so I spent the next hour wandering around our neighborhood, talking to elderly neighbors who happened to be out working in the yard. No one seemed to think anything of me being there, wearing my school uniform, at 1 o'clock on a school day.

Having nearly circled the block, I decided to head home to see if Mom had come back yet. The neighbor whose house was directly behind ours spotted me.

"Bethie," my neighbor shouted out her front door, "What are you doing here? Why aren't you in school?"

My mind raced for a good answer but all I had was, "Holiday?"

"It is not! Get in here!"

Since my mom wasn't home, the neighbor called the school to let them know I was safe. The principal wanted to talk to me to be sure and said they had all the 8th grade boys out looking for me.

I was surprised and sorry. It never occurred to me that anyone would notice if I was gone, or that it would even matter if I was. All I knew was I had been unjustly accused and called stupid, and that was not ok.

My parents were remarkably calm about the whole incident. They asked what happened and told me never to do anything like it again. Years later, my mom told me she also asked the principal what happened and the principal lied to her.

It should not come as a surprise that I went to public school thereafter. I suspect it answered the prayers of many.

It would be another 15 years or so before girls were permitted to be on the altar. Two pieces of advice: Ring them bells, girls. And don't call me stupid.

No Cuts

My husband and I completed our wills, including our living wills and pre-planning our funerals. The goal was to make things easier for his children who will most likely be the ones taking care of the details for the last one of us.

As we discussed funerals, I contended that mine could be held in our spare bedroom with room to spare as I don't believe my passing will be noted or even noticed by most. Jeff, the sweetheart he is, contends I'm wildly wrong, the venue will be overflowing with people who love me.

The discussion made me think back to the death of Pope John Paul II. I was saddened, but I must admit to feeling a bit relieved on his behalf – the poor man had been through so much.

During the last few years, as his body grew weaker with illness and age, he appeared to be sinking under the weight of his mitre and I felt desperately sorry for him. He was once so strong and vital and then struggled for each word or gesture. I imagined him forced to have his frailty on display and worried about his sense of dignity. I wished him peace.

I gathered his mental abilities were not diminished by age or disease, though his physical ailments may have made it appear so. As such, he taught a life lesson about appearance versus reality, about commitment and dedication, and strength and vulnerability. And dignity.

Having said all that, I was interested in those who went to view the Pope's body. At one point, I wished I were in Rome to both pay my respects and to be a part of the spirituality. However, knowing I wouldn't be going to Rome, I wondered just how long I'd be willing to wait in line.

Elizabeth A. Winter-Sharpe

Learning that the wait to file by the Pope's body was 8 hours, I nodded and thought, "Understandable. I'd wait that long." Hearing the wait was 24 hours, I wondered, "24 *hours*? Would I wait that long?"

Hearing that people were taking photographs and making recordings made me sad and uncomfortable. I imagined them showing up on Ebay.

I certainly mean no disrespect to either the Pope or to those who did wait to see him. I'm more curious than anything else. How long would you wait? What's your cutoff point?

Were he alive, I'd wait in line for 24 hours to meet him. Sure. But to see his body? Not so sure. If you'd wait in line for 24 hours, would you wait 48? 72?

Being a fallen Catholic, I'm a little fuzzy on the details but I thought the body was just a vessel; that our soul was the essence of our being. Therefore, the Pope's soul has gone on to its eternal resting place, a.k.a., heaven. Therefore, why view his body?

When we go to a funeral home for calling hours, we say we're there to pay our respects. If we assume the deceased somehow *knows* you're there, then arguably you could pay your respects from the comfort of your own home and the deceased would be aware of it.

We really go to calling hours to comfort the loved ones of the deceased. So, were people hugging the cardinals as they went past? Did they murmur kind words and bring them a casserole?

Were I awaiting my turn, I would have been furious when the US delegation showed up. These late-coming line jumpers were bumped straight to the head of the line. Yeah, yeah, the sitting president is a busy man, and his spouse and secretary of state get a freebie by association. But the former presidents, too? And their spouses?

Tales of the Terminally Awkward

I realize their ride was leaving, but get in line and catch another flight, dude. My schedule is just as important as yours. You're retired and I had to take a day, or two, off work. And you had the audacity to bring a date. Might as well bring the pilot, flight attendants, bag handlers and their driver.

Thankfully, former Pope Benedict and Pope Francis seem to be hale and hearty, but we know this will come up again. In fact, for all our Italian friends who find themselves in line with rude Americans, take the lead from our children who say: niente tagli, niente culi, niente noci di cocco. The original phrase sounds cuter, more lyrical, perhaps: No cuts, no butts, no coconuts.

Elizabeth A. Winter-Sharpe

Alarmed

I rarely hear noises of any sort in my house, but if my husband is out of town the place turns into a concert of creaks, groans, squeaks and what can only be the soft footfalls of the various and sundry murderers who are trying to sneak in and off me.

On more than one occasion, I've woken up in the morning only to discover I had gotten up in the middle of the night and put chairs up against the doors. I didn't remember doing it but was proud that, at least subconsciously, I decided to take action.

My (now) ex-husband used to make fun of me for putting a dowel rod in the tracks of the sliding doors on the second floor. But, as I told him, murderers are a wily bunch.

When I got divorced, a friend insisted I have the locks changed and get a security system. He was very protective of me but I suspect he was also tired of the texts and phone calls asking what a particular sound might be. Neither my descriptions nor my imitations seemed to help him diagnose the cause.

I told a coworker about my midnight furniture moving, despite the security system, and she surprised me with a set of alarmed doorstops. Once activated, if anyone attempts to move them, they emit an ear-splitting shriek that will wake the neighborhood and surely summon the police, fire department, armed forces, and any Mounties that happen to be nearby.

That night I carefully placed the activated doorstops and went to bed, confident my home was secure. I guess I should have explained the new system to the cats.

Tales of the Terminally Awkward

At some point in the early morning hours, one of the cats decided the doorstop was a new toy and nudged it. The alarm went off and, from a deep sleep, I jumped straight up into the air. Based on past experiences, so did both cats. I was screaming; the cats were howling. They ran for cover. I grabbed the baseball bat that resides next to the bed and ran toward the front door, flipping on lights as I went.

I found myself alone in the foyer. Once certain the door had not been tampered with, I turned off the alarm and slid to the floor, my heart pounding, my hands shaking. The cats slowly crept towards me, no doubt thinking I may as well feed them since I was awake anyway.

As I waited for my heart rate to return to normal, I pondered how I could use the doorstops without tempting the cats. Aha! I could cut a shoebox in half and slide them over the doorstops to protect them. I immediately went to my computer and began shopping for shoes. It's not like I'd be able to sleep anytime soon.

Elizabeth A. Winter-Sharpe

Fawks Pass

I was a surprise to my parents; I think "bonus baby" may be the kinder way to put it.

My dad always denied I was unplanned but his take wasn't much better. "We always planned for *four* children," he'd say. "When your mom turned 33, I told her we'd better get a move on if we were going to have two more. But when you were born she said, "'Never again!' She was done."

Sometimes I wonder if I subconsciously believed that as a latecomer to the party I should be an extra nice guest.

My parents were in their mid-thirties when I was born and my siblings were eight and 10. As a result, I was always older than my years. Well before kindergarten, I had a fairly extensive vocabulary, a wry sense of humor and when I liked child-like things, it was in more of a nostalgic way, like, "Aw, isn't that cute."

I was also tall for my age. I think my height, combined with my behavior, caused many people – including my family – to forget I was much younger than I seemed. Basically, I could speak the language but had no idea what I was saying.

When I was eight, several extended family members came to visit for a long weekend. They were all from out of state so it was a rare event. On Saturday night, my sister and a cousin were saddled with me, and they took me along to a double-feature at the drive-in. I have absolutely no idea what movie played first – I'm pretty sure I was face down in a bucket of popcorn - but the second movie was Grand Prix. I remember seeing the title screen and fell asleep about 10 seconds later.

The next day my extended family gathered for lunch and my aunt asked me if I enjoyed the movies the night before. Everyone got quiet and looked at me so I thought it must be an important question. As a result, I wanted to be both precise and honest. So, with all the earnestness an eight-year-old could muster, I responded, "All I saw was Big Pricks."

The high-pitched intake of breath from the women was intertwined with the men coughing as they choked on their iced tea. My mother's face made it clear I had made a grave error, though I believed it was because I fell asleep after they had paid for me to go to the movies. My sister piped up and said emphatically, "We saw **Grand** Prix," pronouncing it "preeeeeeeee."

Never let it be said I don't step up for accuracy because I quickly said, "No, it was **Pricks**. Maybe it was *Grand* **Pricks** instead of *Big* **Pricks** but I definitely saw **PRICKS**, spelled with an 'X'." This time there were loud guffaws from the men slapping their knees and demure giggles from the women holding their manicured hands over their mouths.

My mom told me to "be quiet and eat" as everyone slowly recovered. My uncle noted, "Well, she doesn't speak French," which brought more laughter I didn't understand. Why was that funny? I was eight. I lived in Ohio. Of course, I didn't speak French. I spoke English like everyone else I knew.

I went to my sister for insight.

"Why did Mom get mad at me and everyone else laugh at me?"

"Because you mispronounced a French word that means something else in English."

"What does it mean?"

"It's an adult word, not a kid word. You don't need to know what it means."

"I needed to know it *today*!"

Elizabeth A. Winter-Sharpe

I wish I could tell 8-year-old me that this was merely foreshadowing. For the rest of your life you will consistently say the equivalent of "All I saw is big pricks," and everyone will laugh. The secret, Bethie, is to laugh along. It really is pretty funny. And, maybe someday, you'll write a book about it.

Tales of the Terminally Awkward

License to Chill

There are few moments in your teen years that measure up to getting your driver's license. The sense of freedom, knowing that you no longer need your parents to cart you around (even though you may need their car) is intoxicating. Your license is a not only a symbol of your independence but documented proof of your superior knowledge, intellect and sound judgment befitting your status as a near-free, near-adult. At least that's how I felt...for a good couple of months.

I got my driver's license the summer before my junior year of high school. My parents allowed me to drive their Vista Cruiser station wagon, complete with the wood paneling on the sides. Still, freedom is cool, no matter what it looks like. (At least, that's what I told myself.)

A friend and I would go out most weekends at least once, with or without our boyfriends. That October, the two of us decided to go to a movie. She wanted to see the horror flick, *Halloween*.

I had never seen a horror movie. I had seen a horror *commercial* - for *The Exorcist* movie - and that was enough. It scared the bedaddle out of me, so much so I didn't go into our basement family room alone for months. Even then, every light had to be on.

My friend scoffed as I explained my fear, telling me "everyone was scared of *The Exorcist*" and this movie would be entirely different. Gamely, I agreed to go.

I got through the movie okay, until the very last scene. SPOILER ALERT: The murderer was shot numerous times and fell off a balcony. We see him lying on the ground, clearly dead, sporting his signature blue jumpsuit and white face mask.

I breathed a sigh of relief, my inner monologue chiming in. "Whew! Okay. That wasn't so bad. He's dead. We're safe now. Wow, that was intense."

Then the protagonists lean over the balcony rail for another look at the murderer and . . .HE. WAS. GONE! My entire body went ice cold. This wasn't some supernatural creature, the murderer was human. I thought my heart may have stopped but it couldn't have because my inner monologue erupted. "Wait! What?! He's still alive?! He's out there? What's happening?! Noooooo!"

The lights came up and we made our way out of the theater, turning into a side hallway to visit the restroom. Silent, I was trying to figure out why anyone would go to such a movie, why anyone would *make* such a movie. Then I had a terrifying thought – maybe it was a documentary! It's not like I checked. Maybe they made the movie to warn us the murderer was still out there! I was now on high alert.

We left the restroom. Turning back into the hallway, I looked up to see a man waiting for his date. Unfortunately, the man was wearing blue coveralls and had long, white-blond hair that fell over the side of his face. I let out a scream unlike anything heard during the movie, pointing at that poor man and continuing to scream until he ran out of the hallway and into the lobby.

Embarrassed, my friend tried to get me to shut up, to no avail. The manager came running and, together, they managed to calm me down. Unfortunately, for the manager, I refused to leave the theater without a police escort, until he promised to walk us out to the Vista Cruiser, look under it and search the interior to make sure the murderer was not lying in wait. Luckily, we were in the clear.

I dropped my friend off at her house and made the long, lonely 2-mile drive home. Though all the doors were locked, I never quite came to a stop lest the murderer jump out and try to get in the car. (I mused he was probably friends with that guy with the hook for a hand who murdered teenagers who went parking.) Plus, it was getting close to my 11:00 o'clock curfew and trying to avoid a murderer was not an acceptable excuse for missing curfew. (For the record, I'm not sure there was an acceptable excuse for missing curfew.)

Pulling into our driveway, I suddenly realized that the murderer was probably waiting in the bushes in front of our house. I felt certain he would lunge at me when I went to the door. Even if I made a break for it, I'd probably trip or drop my keys – as all horror movie heroines do – and he'd get me anyway.

Instead, I sat in the driveway and beeped the car horn until my mother came to the door. She stepped out onto the porch and hissed, "What are you doing? Get in this house before you wake up the neighborhood! What is **wrong** with you?"

Some may think I didn't demonstrate the best knowledge, intellect or judgment in this particular situation, despite the validation provided by having a driver's license. I'd concede the point except I knew my mother. Michael Myers, snarky neighbor or schoolyard bully – if my mother learned you were trying to hurt one of her kids, she would Take. You. Out.

I may have lost my driving privileges for a week but at least I knew I was safe in our single-story, mother-secured, murderer-free home.

Elizabeth A. Winter-Sharpe

Drive-In Debutante

My parents were 34 years old when I was born. I'm not sure their age matters to this story but I thought their rules were old-fashioned. Or perhaps my siblings, who were eight and ten years older than me, had caused enough of a ruckus growing up that my parents were trying to kibosh any possibility of the same during my teen years.

As a teen, I suffered from a wildly early curfew, a social life dependent on good grades, and teenage dramatics had to be kept to a minimum. So, on average, a perfectly normal (for the time) upbringing that was horrific to a moody teenager.

And they had one rule that was so ridiculous, so unfair, I was astonished it had even been decreed, let alone imposed: I was not allowed to go to a drive-in movie.

Arguing with the rules was not tolerated, which only bolstered my belief the rules were nonsensical. If they made sense, they could stand up to scrutiny.

I was seventeen. I had my first real boyfriend. He had a car. We were in love and felt like we had the world by the tail! Our only problem was my parents.

Despite my (self-proclaimed) maturity and worldliness, I was expected to tell my parents where we were going. And I still had a curfew! It was humiliating!

One Saturday morning, I mentioned to my mom that Beau and I were going to a drive-in movie that night.

"You most certainly are NOT going to a drive-in," my mother exclaimed.

Tales of the Terminally Awkward

"What? Why?"

"Nice girls don't go to drive-ins."

"Why? What does that even mean?"

"It means under no circumstances is MY daughter going to a drive-in!"

"You and Dad took me to a drive-in when I was four. You let *both* your daughters go when I was eight. Was I not a nice girl then?"

"That's different. If you're going to argue with me you can just stay home!"

We didn't go to the drive-in that night but I hated that my parents did not appreciate the depth of my maturity and worldliness, and were seemingly intent on ruining my life!

I gathered my equally mature and worldly (and, as it turns out, somewhat *less* naïve) friends for their thoughts. Susie summed it up for us, "She thinks you're going to have sex."

"SEX!? At the drive-in?"

"Yeah. You know, you start making out, climb into the back seat and . . . "

My worldliness slipped a bit, "What? People do that? At the drive-in? What if someone looks in the window?"

"Nah, they won't. They're watching the movie. Or they're doing it, too."

Mind. Blown.

Plan. Born.

I would finally prove to my parents that I was too mature for their rules. To do this, I would BREAK the rule, GO to the drive-in and NOT have sex there. (I never thought about how I would tell my parents or prove it. Logic was not my strong suit at the time.)

Elizabeth A. Winter-Sharpe

My boyfriend was all-in. Looking back, I don't think he was all in because he wanted to prove my parents wrong. Just maybe, he wanted to prove them right.

It was already late in the season so we decided to go that Saturday night. As the day progressed, I became increasingly nervous. Crossing my parents was not wise. My mother told us early and often that she would always know if we stepped out of line. The thought terrified me as a child. As a teenager, I scoffed, but part of me still believed her.

Beau picked me up at 8:00 and we set off for the drive-In. (I told my parents we were going to the movies but offered no other details and they didn't ask. Whew!) It had been a gloomy day, which made it seem darker than usual, and there was an intermittent drizzle of rain.

Several cars were lined up in front of us waiting to enter. The ticket-taker wore a bright yellow raincoat with a hood and carried a big silver flashlight. I noted she always spoke to the driver then shined the flashlight in the back seat before collecting the money and waving them in.

I whisper to Beau, "What is she looking for in the back seat? Beer? Rubbers?" As if you would have those items laid out on the back seat. And why was I whispering? Clearly, I was distracted. I had sex, or, not sex, on my mind.

"Don't worry. We're cool," he said.

As each car proceeded through the gate, my heart started to pound a little faster; my palms got a little clammier. I started to wonder, "Do I *look* like a nice girl or like a drive-in girl?"

I turned on the overhead light and examined my makeup in the rearview mirror. Not too much eye shadow. Good. But I *was* wearing Kissing Potion™ lip gloss. Strawberry. Does that help or hurt? Never mind. It was our turn to pay. My heart started to pound as guilt washed over me.

The woman – about my mother's age - smiled and asked how many.

"Two."

Meanwhile, I sat as demurely as one could in the middle of the bench seat of his Chevy Impala, snug against Beau's side. I leaned down and beamed at her through his window, trying as hard as I could to look like a nice girl that would be watching the movie and *not* having sex.

She shined the flashlight into the backseat, collected his money and went to get change. When she came back to the car, she handed him the change and then thrust a handful of paper towels at me. "Here," she said, "You might need these."

What? I knew what she was insinuating! Angry at being unjustly accused, I said, "HOW DARE YOU! You don't even know me. I'm a NICE girl and we're here to watch the movie. We do NOT need your…SEX TOWELS!"

Beau sunk down a few inches in his seat, hand over his face. The woman stared at me in astonishment. She recovered a few seconds later and said, "Sweetie, it was raining. I thought you might want to wipe off your windows."

Oh. My face burned with embarrassment. "Oh. Of course. Well then. Good idea. Thank you," I said.

I hissed at Beau, "Go. Just go!"

We entered the drive-in and followed the lane around the side, across the back and right out the exit. I had told Beau to take me home. Flaunting the rules – even for a good cause - was exhausting.

On the other hand, I had gone to the drive-in and did not have sex.

I never told my parents though. And I've never been back to a drive-in.

Elizabeth A. Winter-Sharpe

Rock of Ages

I have mixed feelings about concerts. I love music and I love to sing (however badly) but I'm never quite prepared for what happens when I go to a concert.

It all started with my very first concert, The Doobie Brothers, who played one late summer evening at an area amphitheater. Unfortunately, I didn't actually see them nor do I remember hearing them, but the evening is seared into my memory.

Beau and I had lawn seats for the sold out show, so we arrived early, and carefully scoped out the perfect spot for our blanket, staking our claim for the evening. As the lawn filled, late arrivals were forced to wedge their blankets between those of the early birds, everyone hopeful that shared musical tastes would make close quarters with strangers enjoyable.

We noticed one couple moving across the lawn, stopping to debate the pros and cons of each spot they considered. Clearly drunk, they were still able to recognize an ideal spot because they dropped their blankets right in front of us and then wandered off.

They reappeared just before the concert was to start, each holding two beers, which they chugged. I remember thinking, "They're going to be too drunk to enjoy the show."

As if proving my point, they immediately lay down on one blanket and covered themselves with another. Imagine my surprise when, instead of napping, they did "the deed," loudly, for the next 90 minutes.

Tales of the Terminally Awkward

We didn't know what to do, nor was there anywhere to go, so we sat on our blanket, trying desperately not to see or hear anything though, admittedly, some things would not be ignored. To this day, hearing "China Grove" makes me blush.

It was my first concert, and I had a front row seat, just not for the performance I paid to see.

Time marched on and I decided to try again, going with a friend to see the Rolling Stones. We were running a little late so no one was in line as we walked up to the entrance. Excited to be there, I smiled and greeted the gate attendant who held out his right hand to me. I didn't remember the attendants being so friendly at my first concert but I was charmed and shook his hand warmly, half expecting it to turn into a hug.

To no one's surprise but mine, he yanked his hand back and said, "Give me your purse!" Indignant, I said, "I will not!" The attendant and I glared at each other as my friend patiently explained the new (to me) security protocols.

Begrudgingly, I let the attendant look in my purse but my glare made it clear we would not be friends. Though he didn't seem to care, I like to think that deep down he felt bad.

The following year, David Bowie came to town. A big fan, I thought it was odd he was opening for Nine Inch Nails, a group I'd never even heard of. Regardless, my Rolling Stones friend and I got tickets.

I vowed this time I would not be caught unaware of the social mores; I would research and be prepared. Unfortunately, Nine Inch Nails was classified as "industrial rock," which meant nothing to me. Regardless, we decided having the right look was half the battle. In retrospect, I should have done more research.

We wore head to toe black, extreme makeup, and fake tattoos, and spiked our hair. Near as we could tell, we fit in perfectly. No one gave us a second look as we walked across the lawn to the area closest to the pavilion, a prime spot to see David Bowie.

Elizabeth A. Winter-Sharpe

The crowd erupted when Bowie first came on stage. Just as the first note was played, someone bumped into me. I turned to apologize, but was hit in the back, knocking me into my friend. Righting myself, I started to turn and glare but was hit a third time. At this point, the blows came faster, from all directions, and it wasn't fists but entire bodies flinging themselves at me.

As each body hit me, I would try to speak, torn between an apology and a stern rebuke. Instead, all I did was alternate keys in an ongoing series of progressively louder yelps.

"WE'RE IN A MOSH PIT," my friend yelled.

"WHAT?"

"MOSH PIT," he yelled, waving me towards him.

Like swimming against the current, especially if fish are adult-sized humans throwing themselves at you, escaping a mosh pit is difficult and exhausting. I was bruised and started to think I was just too old for live music.

Some years later, I tried again with Jimmy Buffett. Parrotheads are known for elaborate tailgate parties; the music is fun and laid back. Perhaps it was more my speed.

My (adult) niece and I got lawn seats for an amphitheater in Pennsylvania. We arrived early, walked through all the tailgate parties, and got to the gate just as it opened. I was ready.

I dressed the part in an assortment of leis and beads, and, so there was no doubt, literally wore a parrot on my head. No purse, I had my keys, cash and ID in my pocket. Unfortunately, I was once again behind the times.

When I handed over our tickets, the gate attendant demanded, "Lift up your shirt."

"Excuse me?"

"Lift. Up. Your. Shirt."

Tales of the Terminally Awkward

"What? No."

"It's the rule."

"How is that a rule? What is this, Mardi Gras? It's inappropriate. I'm old enough to be your mother!"

Every argument I made was for naught and it gradually became clear that we were going to have to put our skivvies on display if we wanted to go in. We acquiesced. Grudgingly.

We forgot our embarrassment as soon as the show began, and we sang our hearts out until intermission when two young men stumbled over to us. Somewhere in their mid-twenties, they were so drunk I was amazed they could still stand, and they reeked to high heaven. We later dubbed them the "Smelly, Drunken Goat Boys."

"Hi, ladies. Are you having a good time?"

"Yes, thanks."

"Here. We brought you a drink," one of them said, each holding out a beer to us.

"Thanks. You're very kind but it's not a good idea to take drinks from strangers."

"You don't have to worry about us. We're third grade teachers. We spend our summers following Jimmy around and drinking. Can you believe it? That's *why* we're teachers." Oh, dear.

The band returned and the SDGBs misguidedly tried to entice us to dance with them. Finally realizing it wasn't going to happen, they simply danced with each other. Worried they might be *lost* smelly drunken goat boys, who would follow us into the parking lot, we slowly backed away, moving sideways to get out of their line of vision. At this point, we figured we may as well beat the rush and go home or we'd be looking over our shoulders for the rest of the evening. And so ended my Parrothead days.

Elizabeth A. Winter-Sharpe

As I reflected on these experiences, I realized they all have one thing in common (other than me): All were at an outdoor venue. Aha!

Once, I took my niece to a concert at an indoor venue and nothing weird happened there. Of course, she was four and it was Sharon, Lois and Bram. Maybe those are my people - Skinnamarinky Dinky Dink, Skinnamarinky Doo . . .

Candy Man

I met my first love when I was a senior in high school. It was so romantic and perfect we considered getting married as soon as we graduated. Ultimately, I refused to get married before I was legally allowed to drink champagne at my own wedding. Plus, my parents would have killed me. Whether I was somehow wise, fearful or just that enamored with champagne, I'll leave up to others. Still, the extra years and experience saved us from what would have been a terrible mistake – procreation.

We both wanted children. Beau didn't care how many so long as the first son would be named Montana Joe. He would be named after the pro football player of whom Beau was a fan, but he didn't want to be a copycat so he reversed the player's first and last names. He wanted another child to be named Dakota and, God forbid, if we had twins he wanted them *both* to be named Dakota and their nicknames to be "North and South." Still, we both wanted children so we took it as a sign we were destined to be together forever.

If alarm bells were tinkling at the prospect of Montana and little North and South, they started to clang when he described his child-rearing beliefs. "They're kids," he said, "So give 'em candy. Kids like candy. They *want* candy. If my kids ask for candy, I'm going to give 'em candy."

Other than the candy plan, he had nothing. No thoughts about bedtime, manners, schooling, discipline, nothing except, "Give 'em more candy."

Much to my surprise, I would soon get to see his plan in action.

Elizabeth A. Winter-Sharpe

We often babysat for a couple with three young daughters: Four, Two and Baby. One night, I was putting the baby to bed and Beau was watching the other two. I left them in the family room for about 20 minutes.

When I returned, they were all sitting on the couch and Beau was reading them a story. I smiled at the sweet image and thought maybe he *would* be a good father. Then I looked again, the real image making its way into my brain. Each of the girls had a bowl on her lap, filled with M&Ms. They were stuffing them into their mouths as fast as they could.

"Beau, what's going on? Where'd they get candy?"

"They asked me for candy so I found some and gave it to them," he replied.

"A whole bowl? Each? Have you lost your mind?" (Though, in fairness, it's not like I hadn't been warned.)

"What? They wanted it."

Four was now more interested in our discussion than the candy, probably trying to memorize it so she could report it to her parents in the morning. Two realized it was an opportunity not to be wasted and began shoveling candy into her mouth like a two-fisted backhoe in high gear.

I took away the candy and began getting them ready for bed. A half hour later, they were both tucked in and the house was quiet. I couldn't believe they actually went to bed without a fuss. A short while later, all hell broke loose.

It started with a wail from Two's room. I ran upstairs only to find her, her bed, her wall and carpet splattered with vomit – chocolate-scented vomit. She is crying and wants me to hold her. Of course she does. Of course, I do.

I called Beau to come and help. We had to change her, bathe her, change the bed, wash the wall, scrub the carpet and get her back to bed, ideally before her parents came home and saw the chaos.

Beau took one look at her room and said, "I can't go in there. I'll get sick."

"Fine," I said, "Take Two, run a bath and take off her clothes. I'll strip the bed. Then, I'll bathe her and you can start a load of laundry."

As I stripped the bed, I heard him talking to Two. She wasn't crying anymore, just snuffling, which I took as a good sign. I heard water running in the tub. Then I heard the toilet flush. Then I heard it flush again. Odd.

"Beau, what's going on? Is everything ok?" I stage whispered, hoping not to wake the other girls.

"It's fine," he responded, "Just getting her ready for her bath."

I didn't put two and two together. The toilet flushed a third time and I noticed the running water was louder, different somehow. I heard Two laughing and clapping. Then I heard Beau yelling, "Aaaaagghhhh! Stop! Stop!"

I ran to the bathroom to find Beau standing on top of the toilet lid, water streaming out the sides. He was holding a naked Two out in front of him as if she was an offering to the water gods. Two was now screaming. So was Beau. I now had my own personal fountain, topped with a man holding a cherub. And audio.

I took Two and asked Beau what in the world happened.

"It's not my fault," Beau said, "Those diapers are supposed to be disposable but it's obviously a lie. Look what happened when I tried to flush it."

"Flush it?! You're supposed to throw them away, not flush them. Turn off the water!"

As I bathed Two, Beau started the laundry, fished out the diaper and mopped the floor. He then had cuddle duty while I cleaned Two's bedroom and remade her bed. She went to sleep and all was well.

Elizabeth A. Winter-Sharpe

Beau and I broke up a couple of years later. I heard through the grapevine that he married and had two sons. Neither was named Montana or Dakota. I don't know if Beau enacted his child-rearing candy plan but, if he did, I'm willing to bet it didn't include M&Ms.

Deliberate Dating

A year or so after I got divorced, I decided I wanted to start dating. I wasn't hell bent on getting married again but was open to a relationship. Unfortunately, meeting new people does not come easy to an introvert and I don't have the type of job where I meet a lot of single men, nor do I go to bars. So I opted to try online dating. Here's what I learned: There's a whole lot of weird out there and a fair bit of crazy.

Friends and coworkers had shared many dating horror stories – online and off – so I developed a very specific list of qualities I was looking for in a potential date.

My first date was with a man I like to call Negotiating Nick. Divorced, one son, Ph.D., professional job, likes to travel – so far, so perfect! On our first - and last - date he asked me if his 23-year old son could move in with me. I said, "No! Why would you even ask?"

He responded, "He lives with me. He needs to learn responsibility."

When I noted he wouldn't learn responsibility by living with another adult, he said, "You're right. How about if I move in with you and he can have my house?" I walked right into that one.

Since that time, there have been many of what I call "One and Done" dates. For example, there was Leering Larry, who actually brought me flowers, then stared at my chest for two full hours. He could not pick me out of a photo array if the picture was of my face. He stormed off when I refused to get "frisky" with him in the parking lot of the restaurant.

Elizabeth A. Winter-Sharpe

There was Megalodon Mike, a science teacher, who met me in the lobby of a very nice establishment holding a Megalodon shark tooth over his head like mistletoe. Why? He knew I wouldn't recognize him since the picture he posted wasn't of him.

There was Non-stop Nelson who talked for two hours straight, never asking me a single question. The entire time I went, "Uh-huh. Uh-huh. Uh-huh. Uh-huh."

There was Cheating Charlie who was a full four inches shorter than stated on his profile and told me he cheated his way through college.

There was Bipolar Bill, Monosyllabic Matthew, and even Sex-Addict Steve, which sounds like a good thing, but try and have a conversation when everything is an innuendo for sex.

Contrast him with Limp Leo whose first question to me was, "Are you obsessed with sex?" I asked, "What do you mean by obsessed?" and he said "I mean, do you insist on having it ever?"

Let's see…there was Weeping William who I actually dated for a few months. He was a very nice guy but he cried constantly, about everything - the sunset, my cat's purring, dinner. It was exhausting.

I had two interesting marriage proposals. Interesting because I never met either man.

Manic Mike proposed the first time he called me, in fact, the moment I answered the phone. I said "Maybe we ought to meet first," and he said, "Ok. Let's see, it's July. Do you want to meet and then get married in September?" I just said, "Sure" and blocked his number.

Freaky Frank also proposed during our first phone call. He had been telling me about the hundreds of guns he owns. I jokingly said, "It sounds like you're starting a militia." He responded, "No, we decided not to start a militia because it just attracts the attention of the FBI and the ATF." Five minutes later he told me he loved me, asked me to marry him and come live on his compound in Washington State. I politely declined.

I want to note what I've learned from these experiences. First, I do have a screening process and all of these men passed - divorced, degreed, similar interests and seemingly similar values. But perfect on paper does not translate to perfect in person.

The second thing I learned was what is really important to me in a date and a mate. Bottom line, I want a man who has a job and TEETH! Yes, I learned this from my date with Toothless Tom. I thought nothing of his serious profile photo until we sat down in the restaurant and he smiled at me.

The most important thing I learned though was to proofread my profile. One dating site had what I call a Cosmo quiz. It asked such things as would your perfect date be dinner and a movie or a walk on a moonlit beach, etc. I did not read my "results" nor did I know that they were automatically posted on my profile. But I suddenly started getting a lot of interest.

Dozens of men, all ages, from across the country and even "across the pond" as they say, were messaging me. Initially, I was flattered and then I received a message that was wildly inappropriate. I responded as such and he told me that, based on my profile, he thought I'd like it.

I looked at my profile and my quiz "results" said I was wild in bed and insatiable! No wonder I was so popular! In fact, now that I think about it, I'm a little insulted I only got two proposals.

Elizabeth A. Winter-Sharpe

Cross My Heart

Years ago, my boss and I were on our way to a meeting. Thankfully, he was both driving and on his phone because suddenly an underwire from my bra shot out of the neckline of my top, hitting me square in the chin. If that weren't bad enough, the end caught the fabric so it just stood there, upright, like I was into extreme piercing.

Obviously, I had to get it out of my top and, ideally, without my boss seeing what I was doing. So I twisted around in the seat, turning my back to him and attempted to remove the underwire.

I struggled because I am a very visual person and have to see what I'm doing. So I pulled things down, moved things over and, let's be frank, pushed things up.

I was completely focused on the crisis at hand and, finally, success! I manage to wrestle the underwire out of my top and looked up only to see that we had been stopped at a light. The man in the pickup truck next to us got quite a show!

I thought it was very nice that he handed me a single out of his window. Just kidding, of course.

It was a five.

Tales of the Terminally Awkward

Car Parts

One of life's tasks that I dislike the most is buying a car. I can research the cars just fine. I can sign the dotted line like a champ. It's the middle part - going to the dealerships and talking to the salespeople – that I dislike.

My biggest problem with purchasing a car is that I don't speak the language, so I'm always faced with questions I don't understand. As an example:

- *How much do you want your car payment to be?* Normally, that's an understandable question. However, when one must negotiate a price, you're basically tipping your hand. I usually say something ridiculous like $22.00.
- *Do you want 4-wheel drive or all wheel drive?* I want all four wheels to come along wherever the car goes. Which one is that?
- *How many cylinders do you want?* As many as it needs, plus maybe a spare in case one breaks, which is usually followed by,
- *How much horsepower do you want?* As much as a reasonably fast horse that's not dangerous. Does that help?

My other problem is my own gullibility, especially when dealing with the occasional salesperson who spins a fine yarn. In one recent vehicle purchase, I was supposed to be able to open the back gate (if I had the key on my person) by "quickly and smoothly" kicking my foot underneath the back end. I was cautioned that my foot had to be precisely in the center. Try as I might, even alternating my feet, I couldn't get it to work. I then realized I looked like I was doing the *Hokey Pokey* and stopped using the back gate altogether.

Elizabeth A. Winter-Sharpe

In one situation a few years back, I was dealing with a salesperson who didn't spin yarns so much as weave outright lies. I arrived on the lot and we exchanged the usual pleasantries.

He brightened when he asked what I did for a living and I told him, "Healthcare marketing."

"Wow! My daughter is going to be a doctor. My wife and I are struggling to put her through medical school. Every penny we earn goes to her education so she won't have any debt when she graduates."

"Yes, it is expensive. What year is she in?"

"Ummmm," his face reddened as he stammered, "Kindergarten."

"She's *six* years old?"

"Yes, but she's really smart and knows she wants to be a doctor," he said, backpedaling.

Then I was pissed and wouldn't trust anything he said. I wanted to leave but don't know how to extricate myself from the situation without seeming mean or rude, a lifelong problem of mine.

He told me he had the perfect car and took me to a seafoam green sedan that looked like the design process had been abruptly halted. With a flourish he said, "Voila!"

I have no idea what make or model it was unless there's one called "Hideous."

"Look no further," he said. "I don't need to tell you anything about this car. I don't need to sell you. Do you know why? This car is **made** for women."

"So it comes with tampons then?" I asked, straight-faced, looking him straight in the eye.

"Maybe you better talk to my manager," he sputtered as he backed away.

Maybe that was a little mean. Perhaps that car was made for women but it wasn't made for this one.

Elizabeth A. Winter-Sharpe

Stranger Things

When I was eighteen, my boyfriend's parents invited me to the family Thanksgiving dinner at his uncle's house. Though Beau and I had been an item for more than a year, neither of his parents had ever said more than "hello" to me so the invitation was a bit of a surprise. Perhaps it was meant to be a warning.

The only thing Beau ever said about his family was that they were a little different. Still, this was an auspicious occasion – the first time I celebrated a major holiday with a family other than my own.

Walking into the house, I was greeted by a loud yelling match between his aunt and uncle about the menu at the first Thanksgiving, specifically, the presence of mashed potatoes. Beau's parents stood by quietly, watching the verbal tennis match, their faces blank. His grandmother stood in the doorway watching the debate while spitting her chaw into an empty deli container.

Finally agreeing to disagree, they ushered everyone to the dinner table. Beau was to my left and the chair to my right was empty. I was startled when a hand, belonging to their 7-year-old daughter, grabbed my ankle – it seemed she preferred to eat *under* the table.

I was even more startled when his aunt yelled, "Elvis! Dinner!" and rounding the corner from the bedrooms came Elvis. Not the real Elvis, of course, but Beau's 20-something cousin dressed in full Elvis regalia, complete with a cape, shades and a pompadour. No one batted an eye or made any explanation. Evidently, he believed he was Elvis and everyone was fine with it.

"I'm going to sit next to this pretty filly," he proclaimed as he sat down next to me and brought his face close to mine.

"So," he said with his trademark sneer, "I bet you're surprised to be having dinner with the King."

"Surprise doesn't begin to cover it," I said.

"How about I sing a little something for you," he asked, leaping to his feet and launching into "How Great Thou Art." I suppose it doubled as the dinner prayer, too, because they all sang along.

It was a surreal day with a child eating under the table, Grandma's chaw container on the table, and Elvis flirting with me. As he didn't seem to be giving out Cadillacs on this particular day, I was glad to get back to my own family traditions.

While I never saw Beau's cousin again, that was not my last encounter with Elvis.

Once, while checking out at the grocery store, the bag boy at my lane started singing "Love Me Tender" at the top of his lungs. While he did not look like Elvis, it appeared he was trying to embody him.

Typically, I ignore people who act strangely but Elvis-wannabe would not be ignored. He pulled my now empty cart out of the way, knelt in front of me while he finished the song with a flourish. Then he proposed.

Flustered, I stepped around him, grabbed my bags and headed for the door. He took the clerk's microphone and started calling out, "Don't leave me, darlin'. My grandfather, Elvis', dying wish was that I make you my bride. Come back, darlin'! We can get married under the balloon arch at the Coke® display."

Though I never saw him again, based on my other encounters at the grocery store, I missed him. To wit:

Elizabeth A. Winter-Sharpe

I was standing in the dairy section choosing some yogurt when an elderly man shuffled up to me. He was dressed in his Sunday best suit and tie, and had very thick eyeglasses.

In a weak, slightly trembling voice, he asked, "Do you know where the meat is?"

The meat department was about 10 yards from where we were standing so I figured he must be a little confused and, perhaps, he mistook me for his daughter. I said, pointing, "Yes, the meat is straight ahead, just there. Would you like me to walk with you?"

With a smile and a much stronger, now steady voice, he said, "Why, yes, I would, honey." He took my arm and said, "Tell me, do you like meat? You can have my meat. Do you want my meat, honey?"

Evidently, he was not so confused but I sure was. What's wrong with people and why must they talk to me? I wrenched my arm out of his grasp and walked away.

I finally changed grocery stores but it didn't help much.

During the COVID pandemic, I went grocery shopping at my new store. I was appropriately masked, gloved and distanced but I didn't notice the one-way-aisle floor decals. In the soup aisle, another customer pointed at me, publicly called me out and shamed me for going the wrong way. I was horrified. I apologized profusely and turned back the other way only to see the decal and realize I had been going the right way.

I said to the woman, "Ma'am, this says I was going in the right direction."

She replied, "Yes, but *I* think it should be pointed the other way." <sigh>

It's clear that strange people are drawn to me, I just don't know why. I might be able to accept it but if I have to "face the strange," stop with the Elvis and send me some David Bowie.

Dinner and a Show

Many years ago, I was traveling alone on my first business trip. When I booked the trip, the travel agent asked which airport I'd like to fly to, LAX or John Wayne, I said whichever one was bigger. She told me they were about the same size.

For the unaware, as I was, saying they're the same size is like saying Akron Canton Airport is the same size as Cleveland - not Cleveland Hopkins Airport, the *city* of Cleveland, i.e., not even close.

Arriving at the airport to return home, I should have known there'd be trouble when they walked us through the airport out onto the tarmac where a double-wide trailer was parked. There were about sixty of us waiting in the trailer, theoretically being made comfortable by two oscillating fans, and a gallon jug of water being passed around with a half-sleeve of Dixie Cups.

A mechanical issue grounded our plane and I was taken by cab to LAX to wait for the red-eye. Not the planner I am now, and far poorer, I had two dollars in my pocket and a credit card that was useless because everything near my gate was closed. I used my two dollars to buy a bag of popcorn and begged a cup so I could get water while I waited for my flight.

This long night at LAX was when I was first introduced to one of the best shows anywhere – *Real Life at the Airport*. The debut episode included my first encounter with Hare Krishna devotees, and a man sitting next to me with a parrot in a cage on his lap. He wanted me to watch the parrot for a few minutes but it seemed odd so I begged off.

Elizabeth A. Winter-Sharpe

Like *Tony n' Tina's Wedding*, I inadvertently became part of the show because I fell asleep only to be awakened by a child with a squirt gun shooting water into my face. When I told her to stop, her parents chastised me for trying to prevent her from expressing herself.

More recently, I had a front row seat to a great *Real Life at the Airport* episode while waiting for a flight at the Raleigh Durham Airport. I got a bag of popcorn and found a massage chair right in the thick of things.

As a plane was about to board – the crush of people already formed – the gate attendant made an announcement. "I've just received word that boarding will be delayed 10-15 minutes. Do NOT leave the gate area. Repeat, do NOT leave the gate area. We will board quickly and we WILL leave on time."

Predictably, three solo travelers wandered off. Ten minutes later, the gate attendant began boarding procedures. In another ten minutes, boarding was complete except for the three people who had left. Over the next ten minutes, they paged the passengers by name at least a dozen times. One finally meandered back and boarded. Two final calls were paged and then the door was closed. Five minutes later, the last two strolled back.

Realizing what happened, they opted to work together. One went to the door, tried the handle, punched random codes in the numbered lock, and then kicked the door. The other went to the window next to the door, jumped up and down, waving and calling out to the captain, obviously believing the captain would unbuckle, climb out of the cockpit and invite them in. They did not make their flight.

The next show began with three people who were clearly going on vacation. Accessorized with straw hats, flip flops, beach bags, and drinks in hand, the only thing missing was a pool float.

Clearly puzzled because their 7:00 p.m. flight wasn't posted on the sign at the gate, they looked at the main Flight Information Display and it wasn't posted there either.

Tales of the Terminally Awkward

Agitated, they stomped up the gate desk and demanded to know why their flight had been cancelled and they had not been notified.

The gate attendant asked for their tickets and kindly pointed out that their flight had *not* been cancelled. In fact, per their tickets, their flight was scheduled for 7 <u>a.m.</u>, *the next day*.

Best show anywhere! Available at an airport near you!

Elizabeth A. Winter-Sharpe

Say It Ain't So

I have a magnet on my refrigerator that says, "I may not always have the perfect comeback but when I do it will be the next day while I'm in the shower."

I know many people can relate to this but my problem goes a little deeper – I keep *trying* to say the right thing in the moment.

My first memory of this is when I was nine years old. My sister was 18 and she had a Cosmopolitan magazine. The cover always included interesting little teasers about the stories you'll find inside and I saw one that said, "The Pros and Cons of Having an Orgy." I asked my mom what an orgy was and she said, "It's a party." The magazine disappeared before I could investigate further.

A few days later I was at my Girl Scout meeting and the troop leader asked who would like to host our Halloween party. In an effort to be chosen, I tried to be interesting and worldly and said we could have it at my house because, "There's nothing my Mom likes better than having an orgy." It was my first embarrassing moment, or as my mother would call it, "bringing shame upon the family."

Sometimes I say the wrong thing because I get too comfortable.

I once worked for a large organization and was summoned to a meeting with someone very high up the chain. I knew her but not well. She was very intimidating and the rumor was she was mean for sport.

Tales of the Terminally Awkward

Much to my surprise, she started our meeting by complimenting my outfit, asked where I liked to shop and who did my hair. I could hardly believe we were having girl talk. Clearly, the rumor was wrong; I settled right in!

At one point she quietly said, "Well, as you can tell, I'm pretty plain."

I responded, "Oh, not at all. Maybe try a little makeup or a new hair style."

Her eyes narrowed and in a clipped tone said, "I *meant* I'm plain-speaking."

Damn it!

Often I say the wrong thing because I get into an uncomfortable situation and try to be funny.

> 1) One Friday, I stopped at a drug store to pick up a prescription. While waiting, I was checking my phone and casually leaned against the end-cap. I bumped a large rack of condoms, knocking at least a dozen boxes to the floor.
>
> Embarrassed but responsible, I scooped them up to put them back and as I stood up, with my arms full of condoms, I came face to face with an elderly couple. They stared at all the condoms in my arms and when they looked up at me I said, "Friday starts the weekend!" They couldn't get away from me fast enough!
>
> 2) I once worked for an organization that scrutinized every penny spent, even nominal purchases like a dozen pens or a packet of letterhead.
>
> I had a wall clock in my office that needed a new battery, which literally cost 12 cents. Unfortunately, the new battery was dead on arrival so I ordered another. Imagine my surprise when the supply chain director walked into my office and demanded, "What are you doing with all these batteries?"

I looked right at him and said, "They're for my vibrator."

He froze, did an about face and left my office. Better yet, he never questioned another order of mine. My boss had some questions though.

3) My now ex-husband had a minor outpatient procedure. Afterward, the doctor told us everything was fine, the test results perfect. He also said, "For optimum recovery, no sex for two weeks." My husband reached over, took my hand and, being very pitiful, said, "I'm sorry, honey." I said, "Wait a minute. Doc, when you say no sex, you just mean him, right?" Ex was not amused.

My "affliction" is at its worst when I get nervous. My thoughts get jumbled and I become tongue-tied so anything can happen.

I met a man at a networking event. He was very interested in my work and we discussed it for quite a while. Over the next couple of weeks, he sought me out at other events, peppering me with questions about my work.

I was recounting this to my coworkers and one of them said she thought he was sweet on me! Newly divorced and far removed from dating, I had no idea. A week later he called and asked if I would meet him for lunch. He said he had more questions about my work so I took him at his word.

I agreed and, indeed, we talked about my work. Again. Then, out of the blue, he blurted out, "Would you like to go to Bible study with me sometime?"

I didn't know if Bible study constituted a date but I got incredibly nervous. I managed to mumble something about checking my calendar and we left the restaurant.

I was so nervous, my mind was racing and I was completely focused on what I should say as a goodbye. I thought about saying, "I've enjoyed meeting with you" but worried it might be dismissive, so I thought about saying, "It's been a pleasure meeting with you" but worried it might be overly friendly. Instead, what came out of my mouth was, "I'VE ENJOYED PLEASURING YOU!"

His mouth dropped open. His face turned bright red. He attempted to speak, instead turned and jogged to his car. I *ran* to mine.

I never heard from my Bible study boyfriend again. Evidently, it was not good for him.

Elizabeth A. Winter-Sharpe

Size Does Matter

It appeared my divorce lawyer was unaware that I got a divorce because he used my married name on my deed, even though I had never legally changed my maiden name to my married name.

I called the County Auditor's office and they told me if I wanted to correct it, I would need to make my own quit claim deed and bring it to their office.

With no advice forthcoming from the "public servants" in the office, I figured out how to create a quit claim deed, took a ½ day off work to visit the prescribed office and take care of business. However, upon presenting my document I was informed that I was in violation of Ohio's 2-inch margin law and had to pay a $20 penalty!

The clerk was not impressed when I pointed out there was at least THREE inches on the bottom of the page so, on average, I met the 2-inch requirement. I paid the $20 fine to avoid taking another afternoon off work.

Thank goodness my tabs were okay. That probably involved jail time.

The "I Do" Blues

My (now) ex-husband and I chose to have both our wedding and reception at one locale and it was lovely. Other than being in a hotel rather than a church, it was a traditional wedding and I vowed to love, honor and cherish my husband. What I neglected to ask was if it meant all the time. Or, for that matter, all at the same time.

My dad gave my husband-to-be some marital advice. "There are just two words you need to know for a happy marriage," he said. "And those words are, 'Yes, dear.'"

I laughed and corrected my dad. "That's not how it'll be for us. We'll discuss our differences, come to a mutual understanding and agree on the best course of action to meet both our needs." Dad roared with laughter.

It took Ex and me three years to pick out a couch.

Each time we visited the furniture store we *did* discuss our differences and often came to the mutual understanding that, should we ever actually *buy* a couch, one of us would be sleeping on it. When we told my parents about the difficulties of agreeing on a couch, my dad would lean over and whisper to Ex, "Yes, dear."

My mom gave me some advice. "Just remember," she said, "They're lost without us, but we can never let them know it."

I laughed and enlightened my mom. "That's not how it will be for us. He's very capable and would just ask me for help if he was dealing with something within my area of expertise rather than his." Mom shook her head.

Elizabeth A. Winter-Sharpe

We got new dental insurance last year. Ex took charge of the plan and switching everything over. We just received a bill for his six-month cleaning. It was $1,200.

My mother warned me. He will not be same man you married. He'll do things you can't begin to understand."

I laughed and reassured her. "That's not how it will be for us. He's so practical and consistent. I know how he does things. I can almost finish his sentences. I can predict his behavior." Mom closed her eyes and sighed.

I came home from work one day to find 24 four-foot fluorescent tube lights in varying shades of whiteness sitting in a corner of the basement. Why? Because one light in the laundry room burned out.

Ex went to our neighborhood Home Depot (where like *Cheers*, everyone knew his name) for a replacement bulb but didn't know which shade of white he'd like best. We had two such lights in the family room, with three tubes each, so he bought enough of each shade for all possible combinations.

Unfortunately, he opened *all* the packages and threw away all the packaging *and* the receipt – so we got to keep all of them.

Each one was guaranteed to last at least seven years. By my calculations, if they all burned out at approximately the same time, there would be light (in various shades of whiteness) until...I'm dead.

And for a long time thereafter.

Tales of the Terminally Awkward

A Night at the Opera

Shortly after my (now) ex-husband and I were married, we decided we would not exchange gifts for our anniversary. Instead, we would go on a get-away weekend to celebrate. He chose the destination in odd-numbered years, which meant we went to Put-In-Bay, Ohio. I chose the destination in even-numbered years.

No matter who chose the destination, I was charged with planning the trip, including places to visit and things to do, with him having right of refusal. The trips were always memorable but not for reasons that could be captured in a photo album.

When I chose the destination, Ex preferred it be a surprise and I was only to tell him the type of weather to expect. He made fun of my packing list, choosing, instead, to throw a copious amount of clothing in a suitcase and hope for the best.

As with every trip we took, our getaway weekend to Charleston, South Carolina, began with an argument about nothing. His anger peaked when we were unpacking at the hotel and he realized he didn't bring *shoes*. According to Ex, I "didn't provide enough information" for him to know he'd need shoes. I simply asked, "Where would we go where you wouldn't use your feet?"

He sat down to sulk and turned on the TV for company. The "Charleston Channel" was on, showing infomercials for wonderful stores and restaurants in the downtown area. One restaurant caught his eye because the chef demonstrated their special recipe for grouper, Ex's favorite.

"I want to go to that restaurant," he said.

Elizabeth A. Winter-Sharpe

"What restaurant?"

"I don't know the name but they have grouper. Call and get reservations."

"I'll need to know a name before I can make reservations. We'll have to watch until it comes on again."

Unfortunately, we ended up spending the next four hours in the hotel room watching the hour-long infomercial loop because every time that restaurant came on, something happened to distract us (phone call, housekeeper, etc.) and we missed the restaurant's name. The fourth time through we learned it was Robert's Restaurant in downtown Charleston. I called and scored reservations for the next evening.

When we arrived, I was delighted to find they were playing the soundtrack to The Sound of Music. As it's my favorite movie, I considered it kismet – cosmically, we were supposed to be there, that night, at that time. Anyone else would have considered it foreshadowing because Ex hated The Sound of Music, its soundtrack, pretty much all show tunes, and most performing arts.

The restaurant was tiny, seating about 30 people. It was subtly lit, richly-appointed and felt to me like an old-fashioned, intimate supper club.

The first inkling that the cosmos might have a rocky evening in store for me was when I opened my menu to find there were no prices. Ex was discussing wine with the waiter so I unobtrusively switched our menus. Uh-oh. Neither menu had prices. Not only that, they didn't have the blasted grouper! Curiously, there were only three entrees.

Only then did I notice the fine print, explaining it was a five-course prix fixe menu with an unspecified price. And there would be entertainment of an unspecified nature. Oh . . . dear. I remained mum. After all, the fine print was on his menu, too.

Ex inquired about the grouper and was none too pleased that they didn't have it, but took the waiter's suggestion to try the other fish offering. Drinks came and I breathed a little easier, thinking it might be ok after all.

A waitress served our appetizer, seemingly turned to leave, but instead, put her hand on Ex's chair, and burst into an aria. She was so loud, the sound bouncing off the walls of the small room, Ex jumped about three feet into the air.

She remained in place, singing her little heart out, for what must have been the longest aria ever composed. Ex recovered from his shock and proceeded to glare at me the entire time as if I were somehow complicit.

When she finished, the audience applauded and she retreated into the kitchen. I was careful to applaud only politely lest she be encouraged to come back for an encore.

Ex leaned in and hissed, "What was that?" Knowing he wasn't expecting to discuss opera, I said, "I have no idea. How strange."

Much to our relief, our original waiter came back, bringing the next course. As he set the salads on our table, I noticed he was now wearing a cape. The synapses in my brain told me what was about to happen but not quickly enough for me to utter a warning. He, too, burst into song. Another aria.

At this point, Ex's face was red and his eyes were narrowed as he tried to contain his confusion and horror, and figure out what to do. For some reason, the space behind his chair was center stage and he was the primary focal point for the performers and the audience. He felt all eyes on him, so he couldn't eat and he couldn't leave. Instead, he began a performance of his own.

During the salad course, Ex rolled up his napkin and fashioned a noose, miming its use. When both wait staff came out with the entrée and sang a duet, Ex took his dinner knife and mimed committing hari-kari. If nothing else, it did prompt the performers to move and turn their attention to others.

Elizabeth A. Winter-Sharpe

The final act was the presentation of the bill. It was well over $120, which isn't so bad if you consider that it was for dinner and a show. Ex was horrified.

"Why is it so expensive? We didn't ask them to sing!"

"It's not about asking them – it's what they do. It just wasn't in the infomercial and we didn't know."

"If you ask me, *you* didn't do a very good job planning this trip."

Say what you will, dude, but at least I brought shoes.

Tales of the Terminally Awkward

Out with the In-laws

I was listening to a young coworker gush about her boyfriend and the engagement ring she expected to receive in the near future. I innocently managed to crush her enthusiasm by asking, "What's his family like?"

Her smile faded as she pondered a suitably polite response. "They're special," she finally offered with what could have been an embarrassed smile or a grimace.

Apparently not done crushing her dreams, I advised her to think carefully. "It's a package deal," I said, "You think you're marrying him but you get his parents, his siblings and their families. Forever."

I feel qualified to give this advice because I did *not* heed it when I got married the first time. Collectively, my ex-in-laws were a carnival who called me "the oddball" because I went to college, had a job, volunteered and was an upstanding citizen (their words, not mine.)

It's not that they were unkind to me; they just didn't know what to do with me. They tended to wander through life, bending the law as much as possible and working very hard at getting something for nothing all the while complaining that life's unfair, an opinion that got stronger and louder with each fresh can of Pabst Blue Ribbon™. So, I guess my nickname is apropos…and a compliment.

I feel compelled to note that my ex was nothing like his family. I believed he was adopted, something his family denies but after I brought it up, they did eye him suspiciously from time to time. I'm not sure if it's because he was gainfully employed or because he married me, but they were definitely puzzled.

Elizabeth A. Winter-Sharpe

At family gatherings, my ex-in-laws tend to pepper me with questions about working life such as, "So you go to work *every* day? In the *morning*? Even in the *summer*? You *can't* wear jeans?"

I enjoyed it when they'd advise me to learn by example from a middle-aged relative who somehow manages to get hired for (and fired from) a series of jobs from October through April, but takes the rest of the year off because, as she tells me, "It's summer and you're supposed to be off in the summer."

My ex-father-in-law was a dear and he seemed to like me although I think it was because I baked him cookies and never asked him for money, both of which were unheard of with the rest of the family.

My ex-mother-in-law was my favorite, not because we had a great relationship but because she was so creative in expressing her feelings about me through gifts.

Before I explain, let me establish a few key points about our gift-giving. Regardless of the occasion, ex-FIL gave everyone $20 and ex-MIL gave another gift. We gave them very nice gifts we knew they wanted. (For the record, I'm not hard to buy for and I always send a very nice thank you note when I receive a gift. And I'm not complaining; I'm amused.)

The first gift ex-MIL ever gave me was the Christmas after we were married. She presented my husband with a beautifully-wrapped box of his favorite candy, which was neither inexpensive nor available near their home. To me she handed an unwrapped refrigerator magnet in the shape of an angel.

"It reminded me of you," she said sweetly.

I noticed the angel had a chipped wing and the glitter had flaked off the one side.

Since my birthdays were either forgotten or ignored, the next gift-giving occasion was the following Christmas. Ex received a gift box of pastries and nuts. I received a bag-holder.

The bag-holder is a tubular piece of pink and orange cloth sporting yellow ducks. It's open at the top and has a cloth handle so you can hang it up. The bottom is elasticized. Its purpose is to have plastic grocery bags stuffed into it for safe-keeping. While my grocery bags have never been in much danger, it's one of the most useful things she ever gave me and I think of her every time I have to deal with old bags.

The following Christmas I received my absolute favorite gift. Ex received a very nice new shirt. I was given a perfume sample, a *used* perfume sample.

"It smelled so good I just wanted you to have it," ex-MIL said, "I only used it a few times."

I suppose it's good it was used since I'm allergic to perfume.

The next Christmas was nothing less than scary. Ex received an air compressor. Apparently out of ideas for me, ex-MIL suggested I go into her closet and choose one of her blouses for myself. I was stunned.

Compared to her, I was nearly 40 years younger, eight inches taller and not nearly as blessed in the "girls" department. The verbal tap dance I did to get out of that one should have won me a choice job as a spokesperson for any sitting president.

As I reminisce about my gift-impaired ex-in-laws, a good friend calls. "You'll never believe what my mother-in-law gave me for my birthday," she cries.

"Oh, whatever it is, I bet I can top it," I reply.

"A clock," she says, "Made out of a toilet seat! A *toilet seat*! And she wants me to hang it on the wall!"

You know, I think I'll call and see about choosing that blouse.

Elizabeth A. Winter-Sharpe

An Italian Tale, Prima Parte

Other than visiting Pennsylvania to go boating on the Monongahela River and a couple of trips to Florida, my (now) ex-husband was never much of a traveler. Ex liked routine and got flustered if anything was different than how he thought it should be. And nothing good came from him being flustered.

On the other hand, I loved to travel and was happy to go without him but he refused to stay home. He said he decided to travel with me because he "enjoys complaining." <sigh>

We traveled a few times before getting married – with varying degrees of success – but they were mostly to the beach where the sun, surf and cocktails helped ease his travel issues. We went on some Caribbean cruises, too, also with varying degrees of success. As an example, it seemed to take him by surprise that, when on a boat with 3,000 people you may have to wait for an elevator from time to time.

He often said his dream was to go to Aruba and stay in an all-inclusive resort. In fact, that trip was at the very top of his "bucket list," so I wanted to make it come true for an upcoming milestone birthday.

Having planned the entire trip but not yet pulled the trigger on purchasing it, I decided to bring it up in case I could glean any more wishes.

"If you could travel anywhere in the world, where would it be?"

"New Zealand," he responded, "I definitely want to go to New Zealand before I die."

Tales of the Terminally Awkward

"New Zealand?" I asked, "The whole time I've known you, you've never once mentioned New Zealand. What happened to Aruba?"

"I always talk about New Zealand," he said, "Why would I want to go to Aruba?"

We didn't have either the vacation time or the money for a trip to New Zealand but before I could even think about what to do he said, "Or Rome. I'd love to go to Rome. It's a toss-up really."

Italy could work.

I planned an amazing trip beginning in Venice and including Florence, Rome, Naples, Pompeii, the Amalfi Coast and Capri. I hosted an Italian-themed birthday party for him and presented him with a travel book and an itinerary. I'd like to say he was thrilled and touched but he was horrified and terrified.

The trip was a few months off so he had some time to get used to the idea and didn't say much about it for a few days. Then the fun began.

He came home from work (where one of his closest coworkers was not only Italian but had traveled to Italy twice) and said, "We can't go to Italy."

"Why not?" I asked.

"Angelo says they don't have good food there and I don't want to go anywhere with bad food."

"Italy is renowned for their food. The food will be fabulous and you're going to love it."

He didn't respond.

A few days later he came home from work and said, "We can't go to Italy."

"Why now?"

"Angelo says they don't have lunch in Italy and I can't go all day without eating."

I pulled out our travel guidebook and turned to the restaurant section, which listed hundreds of restaurants in the various cities where we'd be staying. I pointed out dozens that serve lunch, all near our hotels.

He didn't respond.

The following week he came home from work and said, well, you know what he said.

"What does Angelo say now," I asked.

"He says they don't have bathrooms in Italy. I can't live like that."

"No bathrooms? Are you telling me that Italians don't go to the bathroom?"

"No, but Angelo says they just have holes in the ground. I can't believe that would be okay with you!"

Again, we look at the guidebook, this time the descriptions of our hotels.

"I don't know where Angelo went when he visited Italy but I don't think he's the best source of information," I told him.

"I think you should call Italy and tell them what I want," he said, "And tell them I want to eat at five. Angelo says they don't eat until 10 o'clock at night."

"Call Italy? Sure. I'm on it."

The day arrived and Ex was so nervous I was sure he could feel his hair grow. As was our pre-travel tradition, we argued (about nothing) and were not speaking by the time we arrived at the airport.

We flew into New York, LaGuardia, for a two-hour layover. Our connecting flight was delayed for an additional two hours. He glared at me.

Tales of the Terminally Awkward

The next morning we arrived in Venice. He wanted to use the restroom (there was one!) and noticed that the restroom sign had both male and female icons, and people of both genders were going through the same entryway. He glared daggers at me this time, thinking he'd be sharing the restroom with women. I just shrugged. I was pretty sure the saying "When in Rome... " applies to Venice, too.

He emerged and told me that once inside there were separate, gender-specific restrooms. I whispered a short prayer of thanks.

We proceeded to the taxi, which as you might expect, was a boat. Ex looked around and announced he didn't want to get on a boat, he wanted a regular taxi. I was hopeful that those around us didn't speak English and explained to him, "We're in Venice! Look around – there's water everywhere! A boat *is* a regular taxi!"

He was furious at this turn of events and grudgingly got on the boat, complaining all the while that it was rocking. I contemplated throwing myself overboard but was afraid someone would fish me out.

Venice was breathtakingly beautiful. We disembarked the taxi and had a two-minute walk to our hotel, a beautiful mansion that had been converted. By the time we arrived at our room, he was angry again. The elevator was so small that we had to ride separately with our luggage or walk up.

I thought our room charming. He was appalled because the ceiling was too high (?), the bathroom (HA!) too small and he thought the glass shower door was unsafe because if one of us fell into it, it would shatter and kill us.

I suggested a nap.

Two hours later, we woke up refreshed and I felt a glimmer of hope. We set off to explore; he wanted lunch and then to see the Doges' Palace and the Bridge of Sighs. He loved seafood and I had found a restaurant highly rated for their seafood. We sat at a lovely table overlooking the canal and he ordered *lasagna*. The trouble is, the restaurant was not known for their lasagna and it was somewhat different than

Elizabeth A. Winter-Sharpe

what he expected. He also ordered salad, bread, and wine, all a la carte, and the bill ended up being 90 euro, a fact I tried, unsuccessfully, to keep from him. "Live and learn," I said. "Let's go home," he said, meaning Ohio.

We toured the Doges' Palace and by the time we were halfway through, I was ready to lock him in the dungeon. I fought the urge.

That evening we found a lovely outdoor restaurant, surrounded by beautiful old buildings. Ex ordered sea bass and was shocked into silence when his dinner arrived, head and tail intact. Our waiter, wearing a tux no less, asked him a question but Ex just stared at the fish. Finally, the waiter just whisked the fish away, returning fillets a few moments later. I silently thanked him.

Despite it being a lovely evening and even knowing we had to leave for Florence the next day, Ex insisted we return to our room immediately. Venice was just "too different, risky even." The final nail in the proverbial coffin was when he turned on the television. Not only were "his" shows not on but everything was in Italian!

My sincere apologies to Venice. Only eight days to go. Mio Dio!

An Italian Tale, Seconda Parte

To provide context for this story, my (now) ex-husband and I went to Italy. The trip was the #1 item on Ex's bucket list and I gave it to him as a milestone birthday gift. I have never seen anyone so miserable to get the one thing he wanted most in the world.

The trip included all the places he wanted to visit and all the sites he wanted to see. But…

In Venice, they only had water taxis, the hotel room ceiling was too high, the bathroom too small, the whole city "too different."

In Rome, the hotel elevator was too small, the bathroom too big, he didn't like the bedspread and the drivers were dangerous. (OK, I'll give him that last one.)

In Florence, the hotel *lobby* was too big, our bathroom too small, there weren't enough shelves and there were too many people in the breakfast room.

Until this point, I had tried to appease him, make him happy, point out the positives. Then one more thing happened and it was the last straw. He accused me of having an affair.

Not only was I having an affair, but it was the sole reason I "dragged" him to Italy.

We were in Florence. When I was in the shower, he found the itinerary I had prepared. It listed anything we were doing that had a specific time associated such as train tickets, tours, etc. Well, on this particular day I had tickets for the one thing I wanted to do in Italy - early entry into the Galleria dell'Accademia. Why? According to Ex, it was because I was having an affair with "some dude named David."

David, of course, was THE David, Michelangelo's famous sculpture.

I was unable to convince him that David was a statue. An argument ensued, and I finally admitted to the affair. I told him, "I know David is too old for me but he's hard as a rock!"

Two hours later – having missed my rendezvous with David – he finally calmed down and I convinced him that David was actually a sculpture I wanted to see, and not just because it was a naked man. It was also a turning point in our trip.

I told him if he said one more negative thing, if he rolled his eyes or even groaned, I would leave him to fend for himself in Italy and he would have to find his own way home. I think it was one of the hardest things he ever had to do in his life and he managed pretty well until we went to Capri.

Capri is an island in the Bay of Naples, known for its rugged landscape. Having been there, I would have said it's a mountain with two villages on the side.

Vehicles can only take you so far into the villages and then you have to walk. I didn't know it when I booked our hotel but it was almost at the top of said mountain. We had to "hike" probably a half mile and it felt like we were walking vertically. Ex was dragging the suitcase - though it was on wheels - and I was watching him, eagle-eyed, for any sign of complaint.

We finally made it, exhausted, sweaty and wishing we had eaten dinner before we climbed the mountain because there was no way we wanted to walk back down and back up again.

The hotel – Villa Sarah – was stunningly beautiful and we were beyond thrilled, not to mention relieved, that it had a room service menu.

Looking over the menu, I called and ordered a pizza. The gentleman, son of the owner, said, "Oh, nooooo. Mamma no wanna make no pizza today."

"Oh. Okay. How about calzones?"

"No, Mamma no wanna make no dough."

"Well, what would Mamma want to make?"

"Eggs. Mamma wanna make you eggs."

"Ok. How about some fruit, too."

"Oh, I dunno. Mamma see if there's anything in the garden."

I bet Mamma didn't think we'd notice that the fruit had little grocery store stickers on them. Still, they delivered the food to our room and for that we were grateful.

The next day we left Capri and returned to Rome to fly home. We finished the trip without another cross word - and no other affairs on my part - and overall it was a great time. For me.

As for Ex, while he said he liked the trip, I noticed he never again mentioned going outside of Northeast Ohio. To Italy, thank you for understanding. To the rest of the world, you're welcome.

Elizabeth A. Winter-Sharpe

Spice of Life

When Jeff was wooing me, for Christmas he took me on a trip to the Sandals resort in Grenada. We even had our own butler, Nicholson, who was delightful.

I was used to horrible traveling experiences with my ex-husband, so enjoying myself on a trip without having to be on guard every second was a wonderful, though disconcerting experience. I enjoyed every minute...with one notable exception.

One day, we ventured off the resort to take a small group tour of the island. We visited the beautiful Annandale Falls and a cacao plantation, and enjoyed both. Then there was an unscheduled third stop at a little lean-to that had various types of island vegetation on display. I figured we stopped so they could sell us some spices but I couldn't have been more wrong.

For the next hour, our van driver - a bobcat operator on his days off - dispensed the following medical advice:

"If you have the heart attack, put the nutmeg on it and no more heart attack. If you have the diabetes, just put the nutmeg on it and no more diabetes. If you have the cancer, put the nutmeg on it, no more cancer. You can believe me. I do the Google and it's all true. Never mind what the doctor tells you. Do what I tell you."

I was losing my mind! We were forced to stand around listening to ridiculous medical advice and people were taking notes! Only out of respect for Jeff – and because I was also wooing him – was I able to keep my mouth shut.

Maybe I should have just put the nutmeg on it!

Prescription for Trouble

When I was in college, I worked part-time as a pharmacy technician at my neighborhood grocery store. It was an interesting gig. You knew everyone's ailments, gleaned which doctors to avoid and gained a fair bit of helpful knowledge about medications.

You also learned a great deal about the public. Know this: working retail is a tough gig because customers can be *awful*. In fairness, many pharmacy customers aren't feeling well so we'd cut them a break. But a sizeable number of customers are just asshats.

Overall, I was a good employee: timely, quick and a hard worker. Admittedly, I was sometimes pissy with difficult customers. I'm not proud of that, but it has made me a better customer today.

- I don't tell clerks my life story, especially not when there are people behind me who will just yell at the clerk for taking so long.
- I do not verbally abuse the clerks for the price of anything I'm buying. Unless they happen to own the store, they did not set the prices, and maybe not even then.
- I do not question the clerk about what's in my medicine that makes it so expensive. I got to the point where I just said, "Gold."
- I do not go up to the counter and say "Do you have any of those little white pills?" The clerks wait on many dozens of people each day and may not know your name or what prescriptions you take. There are hundreds of little white pills and sometimes their color has changed.

- I do not wait until the clerk announces the total to dig around and find my wallet and money. I understand that these transactions will result in money changing hands in some fashion so I'm prepared. Again, others are waiting.

We also dealt with a fair number of people trying to cheat their insurance. One brought in a prescription from a DVM – Doctor of Veterinary Medicine. When questioned, he insisted he sees a veterinarian when he's sick. And that his nickname is Fluffy.

Another had replaced his girlfriend's name with his own, again, thinking we'd believe he both sees a gynecologist and has a vagina. Her name had obviously been erased and the medication instructions were to "insert one applicatorful vaginally at bedtime." I'm no doctor but I'll bet that would be some trick.

Occasionally, it could be a little scary. Once a man posed as a doctor and called in a prescription for amphetamines. When he arrived to pick it up, it was my job to keep him busy until the police arrived. They arrested him, brought him back to the pharmacy and, *as he stood between them*, they asked me for my name and address. I told them my name was Esmerelda Jones and I had a cot in the back. <Sheesh!>

On the flip side of the crime coin, once I was working with the owner's son and he told me, quite seriously, that if anyone ever attempted to rob us, I was to refuse to hand over money or drugs. I said, "Make no mistake, I will load their car."

Some of the most interesting times were when the pharmacist stepped out. Whether on a bathroom break or a little personal shopping, periodically they'd leave the tech alone.

If a doctor happened to call when the pharmacist was out, I was to tell them I was a tech and provide two options: either tell me the prescription and I'll read it back to you or have the pharmacist return the call.

Tales of the Terminally Awkward

Once a gynecologist called in a hormone prescription for his mother. When I asked what strength he said, "What do you think I should give her?" I replied, "It depends on how thick of a mustache you want her to have." Luckily, he laughed.

Another time I was on my own, a woman ran up to the counter and said, "We're just leaving on vacation and I forgot to get those wipe things to clean up when we eat in the car. What are they called? Where can I find them?"

Without thinking I said, "Wipes? Yes, there are wipes called Tucks® and they're in aisle three on the left."

When the pharmacist came back I filled him in. When he stopped laughing, he informed me that, while Tucks are wipes, they're for hemorrhoids.

A week or so later, the woman stopped by the pharmacy. She was a bit salty and said, "I asked for wipes for our hands, not for hemorrhoids!"

All I could say was, "I'm so sorry ma'am. But I bet your hands weren't swollen or itchy, so that's something."

She did not seem impressed with these added benefits. I told you retail was a tough gig.

Elizabeth A. Winter-Sharpe

Bra-VO

I've had three cancer scares. My foremost *memory* from those times was pure, raw fear. I remember the word "cancer" leaping off newspaper and magazine pages at me and it seemed to be the subject of every newscast – and it was never good.

The first time, I was 33-years-old and it was one of those rare moments in life when everything was wonderful. My whole family was alive and well. I had great friends, a challenging job, a lovely home and I had just started dating a guy I really liked. Then, during a self-breast exam, I found a lump. Just like that, my whole world changed.

I immediately made an appointment to see my doctor but in the meantime, I started to do some research. One fun fact I learned was that there are more than 30 types of bras. I had no idea. Evidently, my lingerie repertoire needed work.

As I read about the different types of bras, what they do and what they do differently, it made me giggle because I started categorizing people as types of bras: some are supportive, some are not. Some push you up, some push you out. Some minimize, some are annoying, and some always need adjusting, etc.

Despite the fact that the odds were overwhelmingly in my favor, I was convinced I had cancer. That's because I come from a long line of WonderBras®, meaning we make things bigger than they actually are.

Of course, my doctor ordered a mammogram and the first indication of what this entire experience would be like was dealing with my health insurance company. They denied my mammogram because I "wasn't old enough to get cancer." Though grateful to have insurance, I considered my insurance a convertible bra. Supposedly, it could be arranged to meet all my needs but, in practice, it was a tangled mess and I just ended up confused and uncovered.

Ultimately, I had to have surgery. I was instructed to tell my next of kin and since I was single at the time I had to tell my parents.

I didn't want to frighten them so I had a plan: I would be matter of fact, nonchalant even, tell them calmly and concisely. In practice: I walked into their house, they said hello and I burst into tears. This, of course, made me a shelf bra – simple, well-intentioned but just doesn't hold up.

When I regained my composure I told them about my impending surgery and my plan to authorize a mastectomy, if warranted, and I would have reconstructive surgery.

My father was a brilliant, take-charge kind of guy. However, in this situation he was lost. He had no idea what to say or do. I dubbed him "the training bra" because he wanted to be supportive but he didn't have much to work with.

My mother, aka the push-up, was determined to accentuate the positive. She said, "I don't think you should have reconstructive surgery. Because, if you don't, you could wear a smaller blouse size."

When I responded that it was important to me not only for my appearance but for my sexuality, she was shocked into silence. I'm certain it was because I both knew the word "sexuality" and used it correctly in a sentence, not to mention saying it aloud. Remember, I was 33-years-old. I don't want to say I'd been around the block, but I was familiar with a good share of the neighborhood.

My surgeon was widely considered among the best in the area even though his bedside manner left much to be desired. I waited in his exam room, cold and scared, in my paper gown. He walked in and the very first words he ever spoke to me were these:

Elizabeth A. Winter-Sharpe

"Elizabeth, I want you to know the fact that you're even here is a pain in my ass. I don't think there's anything wrong with you, but if I don't operate on you and **you** end up dying of breast cancer then **my** ass is in a sling."

In retrospect, I think he was trying to reassure me, but that day I was struck that he didn't seem to think I might get the worst end of that deal.

He was an underwire bra of the worst kind – a show-through-your-clothes-wire-poking-you-gives-you-back-fat bra – because while he can do the job it won't be comfortable or pretty.

The day of my surgery arrived. I had already registered so I just gave my name to the clerk. She typed something in her computer and said to me, "Oh, you're the breast."

I was taken to my room and a nurse entered, chart in hand, and asked, "Are you the right breast?"

Over the next hour or two, I probably talked to six different people, all of whom addressed me as some variation of "the breast."

I was so out of sorts I just answered that that was my name. I did rally at one point and said to one person, "Well, 'Right Breast' is my given name but my friends call me Righty." It wasn't my best work but it went right over her head anyway.

I decided all those people were bandeau bras – there may have been a slight bit of support but, all things considered, they just left me hanging.

The appointed hour arrived and a man dressed in scrubs entered my room. He said, "Are you Elizabeth?" Startled, I simply nodded. He shook my hand and said, "My name is Melvin and I'm going to take you down to surgery. How are you today?"

I don't remember what I said to Melvin but I remember what he said to me: "I know you're scared. Don't worry; we'll take good care of you." He chatted with me all the way to surgery, shook my hand again and wished me good luck.

What was even more amazing was what happened after my surgery. Melvin happened to walk by my room. I was still a bit drugged, enough to call out, "Melvin! Mellllllllvin! It's me!" He was so kind, he came in, took my hand and said, "Elizabeth, how are you? I hope everything went well."

He remembered me. He stopped to see me. He touched my hand. He used my name. He asked my mother if she were my sister and it made her laugh. He wished me well and went on his way. Melvin spent less than two minutes with me but what a difference his support made. Twenty-five years later I don't remember any other person I saw that day but I remember Melvin.

Melvin was that elusive, perfect bra – the one that looks good, feels good, does its job and is available in your size!

Ultimately, the lump was benign and for that I'm grateful. I'm also grateful for my care providers, especially Melvin. It's in his honor I ask: What type of bra are you?

Elizabeth A. Winter-Sharpe

Inside Out

It was day three of waiting and wondering if my body was a ticking time bomb waiting to implode, spreading cancer everywhere. A little dramatic, but true all the same.

When I was growing up, "mass" meant we were getting dressed up, piling into the family station wagon and going to church. As an adult, "mass" is much more ominous and usually results in having various body parts felt up and scrutinized by strangers to the point that no one's a stranger anymore.

I'm a little worried that if any one of the sundry perverts that wander around my grocery store happens to say, "Take off all your clothes from the waist up (or down)," I'd do it straight away out of habit.

So there I was, waiting for surgery. It was two weeks out and I was trying to pretend everything was fine. I had been spouting off that I was done with my insides - didn't want or need them any more - but who knew my body was listening and would take offense.

Truth be known, my body - at least my uterus – had been troublesome for some time. I was ready for menopause but I had to have a hysterectomy.

I told a few people who happily shared their stories with me. It ran about 50/50 for hysterectomies being the single best thing they ever did to it being the worst choice they ever made. I was just tired of having a period.

I was referred to a new gynecologist and I liked him very much even though we had what amounts to a very embarrassing conversation - for me. I decided to be very professional and pretend that I was in a business meeting. Picture a boardroom.

As I discussed my health history, I was able to carry on a discussion that included such words as "flow" (pretend he means traffic patterns) and "frequency" (frequency plus reach equals a concept in marketing), "mood swings" (of the consumer) and "thrusting" (Uh oh. Ummmm, the thrust of your argument, you say?)

I had to have a vaginal ultrasound ("Take off all your clothes from the waist down.") to determine if I was a candidate for the simpler, less drastic procedure. And that's when it happened. The ultrasound showed a mass on one of my ovaries and the game changed.

The doctor was appropriately reassuring even though I wasn't quite sure I believed him. He *was* very kind. Suddenly there was talk of incisions and pathologists and six weeks off work. I became an automaton, nodding my head and saying nothing - sadly, we were on the phone - and things were wrapped up tidily.

I called him again 15 minutes later as I suddenly had a question. I have no idea what it was now. I called him again two days later, after the weekend, with a couple of other questions. He sounded a little testy but that could have been me because I felt guilty about calling him again.

My now ex-husband came up with more questions but I didn't want to call the doctor again. I had just one more question and it was:

>If you get ice cream after you have your tonsils out, what do you get when you have your uterus out?

I thought it was hysterical. Or maybe it was just me.

Without going into all the gory details, the surgery went very well and I did not have ovarian cancer. The "mass" was actually a shadow from a fibroid (benign) tumor behind my ovary.

Relieved and overjoyed, I had a new outlook. To demonstrate it, I began itemizing the benefits of having a hysterectomy. Most important, I could finally stop.

I could stop counting how many days since or until my period. I could stop having to remember supplies and carrying "just in case" tampons. I could stop considering my period when planning, booking or packing for vacation. Maybe I could even (periodically) stop crying at those damn Colonial Penn commercials, not to mention that poor woman who fell and couldn't get up.

My sudden focus led to math. For example, I added up the money I spent on the copay for my annual pap and pelvic, and the cost of birth control, expenses for tampons, pads, pain relievers and chocolate. I divided my hospital deductible by my monthly expenditures and learned my hysterectomy would pay for itself in 11 months.

If I multiplied that amount by the number of months until I would have had menopause naturally (based on my mother's experience,) I would have the tidy little sum of nearly $6,000.

If I then invested that money in high yield mutual funds, in just a few years I could . . . do all the things the tampon ads say you can do but I didn't because I was on my period!

Tales of the Terminally Awkward

Healthcare Odyssey

A few years ago, I started having pain in my upper abdomen. It wasn't excruciating but it wasn't pleasant. Typically, it would hang around for several days then dissipate. Then it started to get worse and last longer.

After a particularly painful weekend, I decided to stop by the ER on my way to work Monday morning to (hopefully) get a prescription.

Concerned I was having a heart attack, they immediately wheeled me to a room and the odyssey began. I saw a number of care providers but my favorite was whomever put in the morphine IV. It didn't relieve the pain but took the edge off so I could at least enjoy the goings on.

They soon determined that I needed to be admitted to their larger, sister hospital and I was taken for my first ambulance ride. On our way, the ambulance hit a major bump and I reached out to hold on to something. Anything.

Unfortunately, my hand landed on the EMT's crotch. I snatched my hand back and we just looked at each other – both in shock. Finally, I just said, "You're welcome."

Arriving at the new ER, I had to answer a series of questions. Unfortunately, I have trouble with these sorts of entrance exams. Among other things, I was asked:

"Who was the resident on call?" I don't know.
"Why wasn't a CT ordered?" I don't know.
"What kind of needle was used for your IV?" I don't know.
"What was the diagnosis?" I don't know.

Elizabeth A. Winter-Sharpe

By now it was after 3 p.m. and they opted to admit me to the cardiac unit. The hospitalist stopped by about 4:30 p.m. and said, "I want to get out of here so I'll just see you tomorrow." I was appalled, but, evidently, she was not the least bit concerned.

As I was now spending the night, I had hoped to find something to distract me. I didn't want to pay for regular TV which, based on the nightly fee, should be free, so I could only watch the hospital's educational channel. My choices were "Learn How to Breastfeed" and "How to Avoid a Pulmonary Embolism" in Spanish.

After a long, painful night, I called for the head nurse, the risk manager, a quality assurance representative and a patient advocate to assemble in my room. I was in pain and pissed.

I told them I'd been in their care for 24-hours, through two ERs, brought by ambulance and admitted to the cardiac unit and the doctor couldn't even be bothered to see me. I'd been left in pain all night, there was no care plan or testing scheduled. I said, "This seems like the type of care that would interest the Joint Commission." With that, things kicked into high gear.

One of my first tests was an ultrasound of my abdomen. Just before the test was done, my IV pump started beeping. The tech finished the test, threw a towel on me and said "Clean yourself up and make that machine stop beeping!"

When I failed, she punched some buttons and said, "I'm not sure I should have done that, what do you think?" I reminded her that she's the medical person and I'm the patient, and this conversation ensued:

Tech: Well, what *do* you do then?
Me: (for fun) I'm a writer.
Tech: What do you write about?
Me: (Gesturing widely) This!
Tech: I bet it will be good!

Later that day, I had another medical test and this was our exchange:

Tales of the Terminally Awkward

Tech: You're very tall. Do you usually hook up with tall men?
Me: That's kind of an awkward question. I don't really "hook up."
Tech: (incredulous) Really?
Me: Really.
Tech: Huh. I should be wearing a scarlet letter! (I appreciated the literary reference.)

By day's end I realized whatever was going on with me couldn't have been that serious because there was an ongoing stream of people in my room asking for help.

A consulting doctor asked me if I could help his son find a job. A nurse aide asked my advice about a job offer she'd received and asked me to review her resume. A nurse talked to me about trouble with her boyfriend. More than a few talked to me about their unhappiness with their job and the uniform requirements. With props to Charles Schulz, "The Psychiatrist is In, 5 cents."

By far, my favorite part of the whole experience happened when I was about to be discharged. Evidently, the practice was to give patients a parting gift of sorts, typically a branded tumbler with a lid and straw. The discharge nurse apologized because they were out of the tumblers so instead she gave me a barf bag.

I laughed until it hurt. I will be back.

Elizabeth A. Winter-Sharpe

Back to Basics

I always thought my post-retirement job would be driving instructor (or auto manufacturer inspector since a suspiciously high percentage of cars don't seem to have turn signals installed). However, after returning from a cruise, I revised my plan. Instead, I will teach "Lines: An In-Depth Look."

Topics include:

1) A Solution to Aimless Wandering: The Invention of the Line

2) Knowing Your Place – OR – Where to Stand if You're Not in Line

3) You're Not Invisible and Neither Am I: When, Where and How to Get in Line

4) When to Stand Still and When to Move Forward: A Critical Decision

5) The End is Near: When to Have Your Money or Documents in Hand

6) Line or Queue: A Study of Worldwide Application

Those who successfully complete this course will be able to enroll in my basic manners course, entitled: "Please, Thank You and Excuse Me: Not Just for Preschoolers Anymore.

What's in a Name?

My parents did not name me Lisa. When I was seven-years-old, I found this deeply insulting because it was clearly *the* most beautiful name in the world. Since my parents failed me in this regard, I began a campaign to change my name, instructing everyone to call me Lisa. It came to a sudden halt when I learned that allowances were only paid to those whose names were on the list and Lisa was not.

(Likewise, a friend's young son decided to change his name to Scotty. His campaign ended abruptly when he heard Santa might not be able to find him. He wasn't willing to risk it. We all have our price.)

In later years my friends and I would talk about having children and the names we'd choose. Though I still liked the name, Lisa had long since been replaced with "interesting" choices like Ainsley and Raine. (At one point, Raine's middle name would have been Storme. Seriously.)

Then one day I had the opportunity to name someone – me.

When my work was first to be published, I thought perhaps I should choose a pen name. With apologies to my parents, I now understand how difficult it is to choose a name.

Parents *are* warned of the pitfalls though some must admit they never read the memo. Basically:

- Choose a name that's appropriate for a child and an adult.
- The name shouldn't rhyme with something awful.
- Be careful what the initials spell.
- And for heaven's sake, use the name's standard spelling. Your child and all teachers will be forever

grateful. Bottom line, choose a name that won't scar your child for life.

For pen names, it's suggested you choose a first name with two syllables and a surname with one syllable. It should be easy to pronounce and spell, and ideally, the surname will start with a letter in the first half of the alphabet. Seems simple, but it isn't. I gave up.

If only there was a formula for choosing a name. But wait, there is!

Search the Internet and you'll find name generators for various "professions." You answer a few simple questions and, voila, a name is developed just for you. If you're the do-it-yourself type, here are a few of the formulas.

If your heart's desire is to be a soap opera star, use your middle name and the street where you grew up. I would be Ann Wedgewood. Cue orchestra, feel the drama build.

If the soaps are too tame, perhaps you'll want to consider a porn name. Use your first pet's name and either the street where you grew up or your mother's maiden name. (There are varying schools of thought.) Our pets were always male so it doesn't work so well for me but my older brother would be Jock Alaho. A childhood friend would be Muffy Homewood. Both apropos, I think.

If music's your calling, your rock-n-roll name is your pet's name and your current vehicle. My best friend is Mitch Odyssey. I can feel the beat.

Your gangsta name is a diminutive or a title, plus your favorite cookie. My nephew is Dr. Twix. FoReal!

Finally, use "The" followed by your second-favorite color and your favorite beverage. That's your superhero name. Something you'll be to your children . . . **if** you choose their names well.

Signed,
The Purple Mojito aka Lil Chocolate Chip

This Little Piggy

A friend of mine, Buddy, worked for a city water department. He went door to door, entering the homes of strangers to read their water meter.

In many ways, it was the perfect gig for him. He was never an office kind of guy, preferring to be outdoors if possible and moving around. Also, he's never been a big fan of people. He's suitably polite and well-spoken, so he *can* interact with others, he'd just rather not. And, if he has to, he'd much prefer it be brief and impersonal.

Seeing people in their homes being their real, unvarnished selves, was a surprise though and his stories were hilarious. In fairness, most of us have done a fast, creative cleanup when family or friends show up at our door unannounced, but we don't change for a stranger. Right? As my parents used to say in any number of situations, "You'll get what you'll get and you'll like it!"

The meter readers traveled in pairs, each taking one side of the street then would meet back at their vehicle to move to the next street. Most days were routine and uneventful. A few people complained about their water bill or asked him to pass a message to the mayor; most were polite, even kind, just wanting to get back to whatever it was they were doing before the interruption.

Around three in the afternoon, Buddy walked up to a house that was like most the others in the neighborhood: small, older, and a little neglected. He knocked on the side door and waited.

The door was flung open by an older woman. Her hair in curlers, she was wearing a flowered housecoat, slippers and socks. She swayed a little and waved hello with a bottle of Jack Daniels™.

"Hello, ma'am. I'm with the Water Department and am here to read your meter. May I come in?"

"Sure! You come right on in. Do you want a drink?" she asked, waggling the bottle in his face.

"No, ma'am. Thank you. Would you point me to the basement, please?"

"It's right there, sweetie," as she waved at the stairs directly across from the door, "You be careful now. Don't say I didn't warn ya!"

He decided she was warning him about the stairs as they were uneven, and the ancient linoleum had cracked and peeled into jagged little peaks. Not to mention, the light bulb barely made a dent in the dim basement.

She stood at the top of the stairs, talking him through his careful descent, interspersed with swigs from her bottle.

"Watch out! We're not used to company."

As he reached the bottom of the stairs, he briefly wondered who else made up the "we" she referenced, then turned his thoughts to finding the water meter. Suddenly, a horrible screech rang out and a creature emerged from behind the water heater, running straight at him.

At the same time, the woman bellowed, "Be careful! Look out he doesn't get ya!"

Startled, Buddy took a step back, turned and started to run up the stairs, tripping over the peeling linoleum and falling onto the steps. Briefly stunned, he startled as the woman poured whisky on his bleeding forehead, sloshing some towards his mouth, for good measure.

Waving the woman off, he hauled himself up and peered down the stairs where it was now calm. He could hear…grunting? Squinting in the dim light, he thought, "Is that a…"

Reading his mind, the woman proudly said, "That's my attack pig! He almost got ya!"

Buddy got out of the house and connected with his coworker who took him to the emergency room. The cut on his forehead was easily cleaned and bandaged. Whether or not he had a concussion was the bigger concern.

"Can you tell me your name?" asked the doctor.

"Yes," Buddy responded.

"Ooookay," said the doctor, who was not amused. "What is your name?"

"Buddy."

"Good. Where are you?"

"The ER."

"Great. What day is it?"

"It's Tuesday. June…I don't know 22nd, 23rd?"

"Excellent. Now tell me what happened."

"There was an attack pig hiding behind the water heater…"

"Shhhhhhh, of course there was. Let's get you a CT Scan, just to be safe."

I guess the doctor didn't believe that Buddy met the little piggy who stayed home.

Elizabeth A. Winter-Sharpe

What You Talking About, Willis?

Eavesdropping is wrong. I know it. You know it. But it's hard to resist.

I was standing at a cosmetics counter at the local mall wondering if I should even bother with makeup at this point in my life when I overheard a woman ask her companion, "Soooo, don't keep me in suspense, did he get it up?"

"Yes. Finally," her friend replied, "But it took FOR-EVER! Like I have that kind of time."

Woah! This sounds interesting. I nonchalantly inched closer, a little smirk on my face.

"Time well spent, though, right?"

"Ha! Next time I'll send him to your house."

"Fine by me so long as my husband is out of town. Remember last time? I just can't handle them both together again!"

Holy Moses! I manage to stop my head from whipping around, instead try to subtly check out the two women. They looked perfectly normal but this conversation was definitely not, at least while standing at the Clinique counter. I was hooked.

I abandoned the cosmetics counter and followed the women at what I hoped was a discrete distance that would still allow me to hear what they were saying.

Tales of the Terminally Awkward

"Still, I'm glad you finally did it. It's been a long time because something always got in the way. Remember? First he got sick, then you got sick, then your parents visited and you didn't want to do it while they were there."

"Yeah, it's been one thing after another for over a year. The truth is, I didn't want to do it at all. There! I said it! I didn't want to do it, AT ALL!"

"That doesn't sound like you. You used to be all about it."

"I know, but think about it. I knew once we started he wouldn't want to do anything else. It's messy. And, you know how it is, at first you do it all the time but then you lose interest and it's just a chore that always gets in the way."

I shrug my shoulders and nod sympathetically.

"Did the kids watch?" the first asked.

O-M-G! I run smack into a display that I didn't see because I was so intent on their conversation.

"Not at first, but he was carrying on so much that the kids couldn't help but hear and came running. Heck, he was so loud even the neighbors were out in their yards. I was mortified."

I felt like I should call someone but didn't know who - Children's Services? Penthouse Forum? Neighborhood Watch?

"Some people just like to watch."

"I guess. I was surprised that so many wanted to participate."

"Ha. Be prepared, they're going to come by all the time now."

Where do these people live?!

"Well, it's done now. Want to go to lunch?"

"I can't. He wants me to come home. He's upset because his balls are deflated. I think they degraded because they weren't used for so long."

No! That doesn't happen, does it?

"I hear you. The same thing happened to my husband and I still haven't heard the end of it."

"I just have to look at the bright side . . . maybe one of the kids is the next LeBron James."

Wait. What?

"That's the spirit! See, it IS a good thing he put up the hoop and backboard."

Hoop? Backboard? Ooohhhhh.

What were YOU thinking?

Getting Schooled

I have taught part-time at a university for more than 36 years, mostly public speaking with a few other communication courses thrown in.

I'm very fond of my students. They never cease to amaze me and sometimes they're downright funny, though that may not be their intention. Here is a collection of interactions that I've documented over the years.

Student Questions of the Week
"I missed class on Tuesday because I came on Monday instead, but you weren't here. It's an excused absence, right?"

"If I'm not here am I absent?"

"When you said the homework was due today, did you mean it should be finished?"

"When we do research for our speech should we research the topic of our speech?"

"How can you expect me to stay off my cell phone during class if you don't take it away from me?"

From a student who appeared to have had her Smartphone surgically attached to her hand: "How can I be expected to interview a family member when I don't live near any of them?"

Eleventh week of the semester: "Is there something I should do to pass this class?"

Elizabeth A. Winter-Sharpe

Student Statements of the Week

"You can't count me absent because it wasn't my fault. *Your* class conflicted with *my* tee time!"

"I know I missed class but I'd think standing in line to buy Prince tickets would qualify as an excused absence. It's not like I had a choice."

"I'm going to miss class next Wednesday night because my aunt is having emergency surgery that night."

"It is so unfair that *you* grade my presentation. In every class I've *ever* had, my work was *only* graded by other students, never by the teacher. You're so uncool."

"It doesn't matter if I do the work, I'm going to pass." (I couldn't follow his logic but I couldn't wait to see how it turned out. As it happens, he was wrong.)

This farewell message from a student on the last night of class: "Remember, Mrs. Winter, be good or be good at it!"

Vignettes

Student:	(Holding his midterm exam) Mrs. Winter! You told us the exam was worth 100 points!
Me:	That's correct.
Student:	Then why did you only give me 48?
Me:	Because you only answered 48 questions correctly.
Student:	But YOU SAID it was worth 100 points! point.
Me:	You have to give the correct answer to earn the point.
Student:	(Looking skeptical) Uh-huh. So it's not *really* worth 100 points.
Student:	Mrs. Winter, no offense but I don't think you're qualified to judge my delivery.
Me:	Oh? Why?
Student:	Because I was great and I didn't notice you watching me.
Me:	Hmmm, I'm glad you told me as I noted your delivery is "excellent" and you have the highest scores.

Tales of the Terminally Awkward

Student: Oh. Well, obviously, you are *very* qualified.

Student: Mrs. Winter, have you given any thought to how we'll deliver speeches tonight? Do you have a plan?
Me: Yes, I do. Remember, I've taught for 30-some years. Not my first rodeo.
Student: Okay, I just want to be sure you have a plan before we get started. We want class to go smoothly, don't we?

(I'm a little annoyed that he would ask such a thing yet a little touched that he cared.)

Student: Why didn't you give me all the points for this assignment?
Me: Because you only turned in half of the assignment and what you did turn in was incomplete.
Student: (Incredulous) You mean we have to turn in the whole assignment to get all the points?

Student: Why didn't you give me any points on this homework?
Me: Because it wasn't the homework I assigned.
Student: But I didn't know what homework was assigned so I did this.
Me: The homework is listed in your syllabus and we went over it three different days in class.
Student: But you have to give me the points because I did work.

Student: My friends ask me why I took this class when you're such a hard teacher.
Me: What makes me a "hard" teacher?
Student: Because if we want an A on our work, we have to turn it in on time AND we have to do a good job.

Student: Mrs. Winter, you look really nice tonight.
Me: Thank you.
Student: I was just saying to (a classmate), "Mrs. Winter looks so nice tonight. Her clothes match and everything."

Elizabeth A. Winter-Sharpe

Student 1:	Mrs. Winter, you look REALLY nice tonight.
Me:	Thank you.
Student 2:	No, really, you look HOT, Mrs. Winter.
Me:	Your speeches have been graded, folks.
Students:	Oh. Never mind.

Student:	I love history.
Me:	What period interests you most?
Student:	The 1980's.
Me:	Do you mean the 1880's?
Student:	No, the 1980's. I'm fascinated by how people lived back then.
Me:	I'm a historical relic.
Student:	Yup.

Student:	For my persuasive speech, I want to persuade my audience that mermaids are real.
Me:	Do you have any credible sources to offer as support?
Student:	Uh, did you ever hear of movie *The Little Mermaid*?
Me:	<sigh>

Student:	I've looked over the syllabus and have made you a list of the assignments I'm willing to do.
Me:	Let the games begin!

Tidbits

One of my students called me "Mom" by accident. It was a first. Later that semester, the same student came up to me. She had put on her jacket and was holding one side out towards me. She said, "Look. My zipper broke. Will you fix it?"

TEACHER question of the week: "When I speak, what is it that you hear?"

Students who couldn't figure out how to use the syllabus suddenly become lawyers when final grades are posted.

Tales of the Terminally Awkward

Note to self: In the unit about "appropriate communication," discuss oversharing. This change was the result of a minor speech in which students were to introduce themselves to their classmates. One student told the class she's into pain and another told us she and her husband are into role-playing games.

A police officer walked into my class tonight and announced, "I'm looking for Elizabeth Winter." What struck me was that not one of my students looked even remotely surprised. (To close the loop, everything was fine. Strangely enough, he was delivering a message for a student that she would be late to class. Another first.)

As I waited for my class to begin, I reflected on my years of teaching and thought student behavior hasn't really changed over the 36 years I've taught. Then a young man entered class and bowed to me. So that's new.

Elizabeth A. Winter-Sharpe

Ode to Dead Appliances

'Twas the day before Christmas
and we had to wonder,
which of the appliances
was next to go under.

'Twas the stove on Thanksgiving,
the microwave, too.
'Round Labor Day was when
the dishwasher blew.

July 4th was different,
still costly, no doubt.
Professionals were needed
to get carpet stains out.

It began when we moved,
just last May.
The A/C died,
Happy Memorial Day!

What could be next?
What will we do?
'Bout the dryer, the furnace,
or the chimney and flue?

But all seems well
and we cautiously smile.
The streak is over -
we'll go forth in style!

But with the flip of a switch,
the shrapnel, it flies.
The mystery is solved,
it's the disposal that dies.

Tales of the Terminally Awkward

The streak, it continues
and the New Year is nigh.
He's developed a twitch
and there's a tear in my eye.

Never fear, we're ok.
We're having fun.
I poured him a bourbon
and he poured me a rum.

Merry Christmas!

Elizabeth A. Winter-Sharpe

Quickies

Philosophy
- Some people are like seasonal allergies. They probably won't kill you but they make you miserable and you just cannot get rid of them!
- Being old enough to know better makes for some awkward moments.
- I'm more successful in my dreams than I am in real life. That would be sad but I always dream someone is trying to murder me and I escape, so that's good.
- Patience is a virtue but it's not one of mine.
- I have no idea how to throw away a trash bin.
- What do you do if you're experiencing the rare and serious side effects but are not taking the medicine?
- Some people avoid leaps of logic like they're aerobic.
- I'm so blue. Food coloring mishap.
- Some days I amaze myself. This is not one of those days.
- I'm such a baby. I went to sleep at 7 o'clock, but didn't sleep through the night.
- I'm not proud to admit this but I feel vaguely satisfied when I use up the shampoo and conditioner on the same day.
- If there's anything more frightening than a magnifying mirror I don't know what it is. Except maybe a spider in a magnifying mirror.
- I decided to audition for the Vagina Monologues. For the uninformed, it does NOT involve ventriloquism.
- I'm in such a great place right now I'm terrified. Then again, Dairy Queen will do that to a person.
- Spontaneity is so important I plan for it.

Tales of the Terminally Awkward

Grands
- I picked up my 4-year-old granddaughter from school. As we traveled to my house she asked after the cats, she asked about my allergies, she asked what activities were planned for the weekend (yes, she said activities) and then out of the blue asked how babies are made. I'm sorry to say I choked and started talking about the traffic. I was not prepared for the ropes course.
- Two of our granddaughters informed me tonight that they like my name, "Beth Snowflake Sharpe." I believe "Snowflake" is due to my maiden name (Winter) rather than a commentary on my political views.
- My grandmother used to say nothing good happens after midnight. I'm a modern grandma so I will tell my grandchildren nothing good happens before 10 a.m.

Money Matters
- Here's a million dollar idea: we should be able to register grocery store items that they will NOT sell us no matter how much we beg.
- I like to think of myself as reasonably intelligent but I have yet to master those damn plastic bags in the produce section.
- I don't normally say this sort of thing but my ability to rationalize the purchase of shoes impresses even me.
- I know I don't have "f*** you" money. How much is "bite me" money?
- My husband doesn't understand how it is I went to buy a couple of things for the bridal shower I'm hosting and came home with supplies to paint our bedroom.
- While shopping tonight I asked for a dressing room and the clerk asked for my name so she could write it on the wall outside the door. Not a fan of the practice, I leaned in and whispered, "I'm incognito". She leaned in and said, "How do you spell that Ms. Cognito?"

- After a lousy day, I wasn't up to cooking dinner so I called a restaurant and ordered carryout. I arrived to pick it up (in a torrential downpour, I might add) and the hostess said, "I didn't put your order in because I didn't think you really wanted it."
- Great news! I received an email from Mr. Jim Ovia Lawosn (sic) that, for my convenience, the Federal Reserve Board of New York has decided to move my $10.5 million to Zenith Direct Online Bank. All I have to do to access the money is send my local bank account information and they'll do all the work to connect the two accounts for me. Great customer service! I had completely forgotten about that money, too!
- Dear Giant Eagle: In this season of joy and giving, would it kill you to card me just once when I buy alcohol? Seriously, throw me a bone.
- On Bahnhofstrasse in Zurich, I passed Cartier, Tiffany's, Jimmy Choo, and more. I saw a GORGEOUS purse, 340 Swiss Francs. I left but began rationalizing. I convinced myself to buy it and went back before reason raised its ugly head. I missed the comma - it was 3,400! It stayed in Zurich. #wearyourglasses
- I'm so depressed. Waiting for a prescription at Drug Mart and every song playing in the store is on my IPod. Except, of course, the Discount Drug Mart song, which is rude on my part because, as the song says, "Discount Drug Mart saves me the run around."
- I was shopping in D.C. before meeting a friend for dinner. I stopped in a shoe store and, not finding any, asked the clerk if they carried "footies." He looked down his nose at me and haughtily said, "FOOTIES? I believe you mean *Ankle Sockettes*." All I could say was, "Dude. This is a Payless."
- I got carded last night for the first time in many, many years. Sounds nice but as it happens I was at Target buying Nyquil. Clearly, I don't look so much youthful as like a drug addict.
- I use my Mastercard for every purchase to earn air miles to pay for travel. At the rate I'm going, in about two months I should be able to buy Europe.

Tales of the Terminally Awkward

- Based on the amount of business I do with Capital One, I'm a little surprised the CEO hasn't asked to connect with me on LinkedIn.

Healthcare
- I had to get a COVID test prior to a medical procedure. Waiting in my car, the medical professional said I looked like a bank robber. She clarified it by saying it wasn't my mask and sunglasses but because I have "bank robber hair." I don't know what that means.
- I gave blood to be a registered bone marrow donor. I received a letter from the registry asking me to participate in a 5K run. Evidently, DNA doesn't tell everything about a person.
- I attended a Chamber of Commerce event and thought I recognized the man sitting across the table from me. I couldn't be sure because I wasn't wearing my glasses. I told him he looked familiar and, lo and behold, it was my eye doctor. Awkward!
- My doctor's office was setting up their electronic medical records and asked if I have a nickname I go by. My doctor now addresses me as "Your Highness."

Travel
- Nothing says I'm back in Ohio like the inability to breathe.
- I received a holiday card from one of the touring companies I used in Austria. Evidently, they have forgiven me for my solo sing-along on their Sound of Music tour.
- Today I learned about the Marie Kondo theory of packing a suitcase. The mechanics seem promising but we're supposed to smooth our clothes so "they feel our love and appreciation." And before stowing our suitcase after vacation, we're supposed to "thank it for its part in making our journey successful." Woefully lacking in yet another of life's arenas, I offer this to my purse: "From one old bag to another, thanks for all you do!"

- Being directionally challenged, I appreciate the convenience of Google maps and the like. But why do they tell me things like "Go East" or "Head North?" I don't know what that means. I use them so often that by now they should know to tell me things like, "Turn left at the McDonalds, go past the shoe store, and it's across the street from that gas station that's always so crowded." Is that so hard?
- Look out world, I have officially been deemed a "trusted traveler." What rights and benefits are bestowed upon me due to this status? Will there be trumpets playing as I walk through the airport? Rose petals strewn in my path? Helpers to carry my carry on? I await my due.
- I spent two miles and 30 minutes next to the same vehicle on the road today. He had his windows down and music BLARING. Surprisingly, it was polka music.
- To whomever invented the pool swim-up bar: bravo, my friend. Bravo.

Home
- I finally cleaned out my clothes closet. I was going to be ruthless but at the end of the day I was only a little snotty.
- Our condo developed an unexpected "water feature" in the laundry room. As we're not water feature people (at least in the laundry room), we hired a contractor to repair it. The repairman said it was operator error, started a cycle to show me how it's properly done and left. 45-minutes later we had a TWO-STORY water feature since the leak became a flood with standing water in the laundry room that flowed through the floor into the finished basement ruining tiles and shorting out a light. NOW HIRING: Cabana boy, part-time, flexible hours, bartending skills and lifeguard training required.
- Dinner with a side of judgment: I ordered a pizza and the delivery man said, "You should have made better landscaping choices." He pointed to a bush and said, "I don't like that one! It has thorns! I could get hurt if I touched it!" I could only reply, "Keep your hands out of my plants, pizza boy!"

Observations of Others

- I saw a man walking down the street this afternoon wearing a skully, a very nice leather jacket, no shirt, swim trunks and flip flops. And I thought, "There's a man who's cracked the code for Ohio weather!" Well done, sir. Well done!
- I saw a guy today with three lit cigarettes hanging out of his mouth and a beer in hand. All I could think was, "Some days, I totally get that."
- No matter what song I ask for, Siri always plays "Everybody Wang Chung Tonight." It may not be cool to out her publicly but I think she drinks. On the job.
- If one could make money by being annoying, I'd know at least one billionaire!
- Overheard in a restaurant from a woman in her sixties (with her husband and another couple): "We couldn't believe it but our daughter-in-law got a job as a finance manager with [big company.] I mean, she has her master's but you know how women are with money . . . I guess she must be good with people." Pardon me while I check to see what year this is and try to keep my mouth shut.

Just Me

- I glued my fingers together twice tonight so I took away my super glue privileges.
- One night I hemmed two pairs of slacks while watching *Project Runway* so I felt like a contestant. Predictably, Nina found my work boring and not fashion forward.
- I stopped at the pet store to pick up some cat cereal (dry food). I had to tilt the bag towards the light to read whatever it was I thought important. I did not notice that some joker had opened the bag so it poured into my open purse and all over the floor. Predictably, I panicked and hastily tried to empty it out of my purse and push it out of the aisle before someone happened by. SURPRISE, today I found a stash of cereal in the inner pockets. So it would appear I've now vandalized, littered, and shoplifted, all in one day, without even trying.

- While shopping at Harry & David's, I noticed a man was staring at me. He said, "I'm sorry for staring. I thought you were my cousin Mary." I said, "I AM Mary!" Invited for Thanksgiving - SCORE!
- When I was about seven years old, I asked my 16- and 17-year-old siblings why people in the movies kissed with their mouths open. They told me the people were trading gum. For years, if anyone offered me gum I would knowingly say, "Ok, but I'm not going to trade it with you!"
- On my first solo trip, I was arranging dinner with a friend who was going to pick me up at my hotel. I told him my room number – 416 – and he asked, "What's it under?" I responded, in all seriousness, "516."
- I've still got it! I went out with a friend last night and we closed the place down. They actually asked us to leave. Of course, it was a Bob Evans.
- In my family, when it's time to leave we say, "Get your bonnet on." I don't know if it's a great code but I love that about my family.

Don't Call Us, We'll Go Broke

Jeff and I went on a Mediterranean cruise and received a souvenir in the mail about two weeks after we got home - a $500+ phone bill! We stayed at hotels with free WiFi, paid for unlimited internet on the ship, made no phone calls, sent about five texts AND Jeff has an international plan. We thought we had all bases covered and called our carrier to dispute the bill. We learned the following:

1) The international plan is only for use FROM the U.S., not into the U.S. (I'm sorry, what?)

2) The international plan only includes Canada and Mexico. (What does "international" mean again?)

3) For places other than Canada and Mexico, we had to get the international international plan. (Of course.)

4) We should have known to ask what countries the international plan covered OR should have known to ask for the international international plan. (Sure, our mistake.)

5) They would not credit our bill because they "only charged the usual price of the international international plan," which we would have paid anyway had we purchased the right plan in the first place. (Sure, that seems fair.)

6) We're such nice people that instead of crediting the phone bill, they gave us $50 per month off our TV bill for the next 12 months, meaning we've been getting screwed on the TV bill all along, too.

The most important lesson: It's. All. A. Scam.

Elizabeth A. Winter-Sharpe

Confessions of a Would Be Rum Runner

Several years ago, my (now) ex-husband and I visited St. Croix. It's a beautiful island and we had a wonderful time, augmented with delightful rum drinks. We soon learned that rum – in fact all alcohol – was cheap: a fifth of rum was $2.60, Chivas was $10. We also learned that each visitor could take six bottles of alcohol home if two were made in the Caribbean. While I don't care much about booze, there's little I like better than a bargain.

With great choices and low prices, we shopped with abandon, not realizing until packing for home that we had 13 bottles.

Ex was unconcerned. I was worried. What if I get caught? Will I go to jail? Will it make the newspaper? What will the neighbors think? (It never crossed my mind to leave a bottle behind.)

Like George Washington, I cannot tell a lie. To clarify, I'm *capable* of lying but I always fess up because my conscience won't allow otherwise. But I decided to be a wild woman, a scofflaw, and packed my illegal $2.60 bottle of island rum.

Arriving at the airport to return to home, my heart started to beat a little faster.

In line for security – a lone man standing at the door to the tarmac – my heart started to *pound*.

Three people were ahead of me and the agent asked the first a question.

"What did he ask her?" I whispered to Ex.

Tales of the Terminally Awkward

"He asked if she enjoyed herself."

"What do you think he meant by that?"

Ex rolled his eyes. I started to sweat.

Two people are ahead of me. The agent gestures to the man's carry-on, tags it and sets it aside. My hands started to shake.

One person is ahead of me. The agent asks the elderly woman a question I don't hear. He waves someone over who picks up her bag and escorts her out to the tarmac. I think they must be taking her to jail. I was near tears.

It was my turn. The agent smiled broadly and held out his hand for my ID and declaration form. I handed it over, careful to maintain eye contact and an unconcerned smile. Unfortunately, I looked like a slightly addled caffeine freak.

He asked if I enjoyed St. Croix and my throat was so dry I could only squeak.

The agent handed back my ID and said, "Have a nice flight," to which I responded by throwing my hands up in the air and shrieking, "I confess!" His jaw dropped open and he asked, "To what?"

My confession tumbled out in a rush. "I have an extra bottle of rum. I'm sorry! I miscounted. Really! I never break the law. It's island rum. Take it! I'm sorry! Will I go to jail?"

Embarrassed by the scene, Ex dropped back and joined some other passengers.

The agent started to laugh. He called over a coworker, whispered in her ear and she started to laugh. I was oblivious, busy deciding if I should use my one phone call for an attorney or a priest.

He handed back my ID and said, "Thank you for visiting St. Croix. *Please* come back."

I didn't move, unsure what had just happened. Slowly, I realized I wasn't headed for the big house. I thanked him profusely and promised I'd been scared straight. I was about to hug him when Ex grabbed my arm and steered me out the door, shaking his head and looking pained.

A short while later, airborne, I breathed a sigh of relief that my brush with the law was over. And though I've been back to St. Croix several times I've never bought another bottle of rum. Clearly, I've had enough.

Making a Meal out of a Snack

Hearing the phrase "be prepared," most think of the Boy Scouts. I think of my good friend, Elsi. For her, it's not just an expression but a way of life. She's a wealth of knowledge, supplies and good advice for any conceivable situation.

When Elsi takes on a task – any task – she will research every aspect including its origins, evolution, methodologies, pros and cons, availability (within a 50-mile radius) and cost comparisons for all materials. All of this information will be recorded in a sortable and searchable Excel file. Mind you, one such task was making holiday hair bows for her infant granddaughter. On the other hand, they were the finest and prettiest hair bows you could ever hope to see.

A few years ago, Elsi and I took a weekend trip to Toronto. We made the six-hour drive after work on Friday because we were under the delusion that we were still young enough to go out after 11 at night, enjoy a full evening of festivities and still get up early to see the sights.

I was surprised by the amount of baggage Elsi had for a 48-hour trip, 12 of which would be spent in the car. Then again, I'd been known to pack for a camping trip with the motto, "You never know when you'll be asked to a prom," so I didn't comment. (OK, that's not true. I don't go camping. But I have taken a prom dress on a beach vacation where the dressiest restaurant requires wearing fairly clean cutoffs.)

Arriving at the Delta Chelsea Hotel in Toronto (thoroughly researched and recommended by Elsi) we went upstairs to get settled before hitting the town. Elsi produced a huge box containing roughly 48 drawers and placed it on the vanity in the bathroom. I was curious but didn't ask.

Elizabeth A. Winter-Sharpe

A short while later I mentioned that I had a little headache. Elsi said, "I have aspirin. Would you like regular, baby or buffered? Or would you prefer acetaminophen? Or ibuprofen?"

"You have all those?"

"Yes. Why?"

"No reason."

"Would a sinus mask help? Or maybe a soothing tape of a babbling brook?"

Later, when responding to various parts of our conversation, she offered up ear plugs, duct tape, scented magic markers and AAA batteries. I realized the box in the bathroom was a treasure trove suitable for *Let's Make a Deal*.

I decided to put her to the test.

"Hmmm, I could use a mint."

"Altoid, Tic Tac or Junior?" Elsi asked.

"You know, I would put my hair up if only I had some bobby pins," I mused.

"I have black, brown and rhinestone-studded," she offered.

"My ankle is a little sore."

"Bandage, brace or balm?"

"I'd like to mark the city map with the places we're going tomorrow."

"Highlighter, sticky notes or rubber stamp?"

"Rubber stamp."

"Star, X, checkmark or pointing finger? And what color ink? Black, blue, red, purple, orange or green?"

While deciding if my next request would be for an embroidery hoop or a buffalo head nickel, an alarm went off (some twit pulled the fire alarm as a joke) and we had to evacuate the hotel. I grabbed my purse and headed for the door. Elsi grabbed a first aid kit and what I suspect was an AED.

Not long ago we were reminiscing about the trip and I teased her about her extensive research and ultra-preparedness for anything and everything. I tell her she makes a meal out of every snack.

She's good-natured and denies that she does any more research or is any more prepared than the average person. (Evidently, I'm below average.) She then goes on to "confess" that she has an Excel file to track her toilet paper purchases.

I laugh until I cry.

Somewhat annoyed, she tells me, "This is serious. There's a toilet paper conspiracy. The packages may say you're getting twice the quantity but when you compare square size, weight and length of the roll, you're not. It's a scam and it must be exposed!"

So toilet paper manufacturers be warned. Elsi is on the job and she *will* squeeze the Charmin!

Elizabeth A. Winter-Sharpe

A Strange New World

Winter's Log, Star Date 62713: Demise of a credit card: Roughly 15 hours before summer trip begins, Capital One alerts me of suspected fraudulent charges on my credit card. Upon my confirmation, credit card is cancelled. New card will be sent to vacation destination via overnight mail. Curiously, it will take 2-3 days.

Winter's Log, Star Date 62713.1: Day 1 without a credit card: Filling up the car's gas tank is a strange experience. The machine that just last week was so open and accepting is now strange and remote. How does one pay for gas without a credit card? I feed cash into the card slot but it is abruptly rejected. I examine the machine closely, trying in vain to find another way. A stranger at the next pump notices my confusion and locks herself in her car. I go into the store to ask for help. The clerk gently suggests I give her my cash and she will take care of it. Thank you, kind soul.

Winter's Log, Star Date 62813: Day 2 without a credit card: Checking into a hotel, I am comforted by the fact that the room was paid for two weeks ago. Today I will not be judged for my lack of credit card. Alas, the clerk asks to "run" my card. As I explain that I don't have a credit card, her attitude changes into one of derision. I show her the letter from Capital One that explains I was defrauded but am of sterling character with another card being overnighted to me, due to arrive in 2-3 days. She is unmoved. In a last ditch effort, I give her my "former" card. She eyes me suspiciously and examines the card. Begrudgingly, she allows me to stay with a stern warning that she is breaking the rules and I'd better not make her sorry. I vow to go back one day. I will have a credit card. And it will be platinum.

Winter's Log, Star Date 62913: Day 3 without a credit card: Cautiously optimistic. Final destination is just three hours away. Car's tank is full, the hotel breakfast complimentary. I can slip through the credit card world unnoticed. Two hours later my spirits plummet – it's a Coach Outlet store, windows papered with 50% off signs. Cannot resist. Must stop. My eyes are drawn to the bag: butter-soft leather, delicate pleats, interior pockets and a shoulder strap; $598 before the discount. There is one left. With a credit card, it would already be mine. I hold it close, stroking the leather, then settle for the one thing I can buy: a cloth credit card holder for $23.99. Back in my car, I clutch my new credit card holder and quietly sob at the irony.

Winter's Log, Star Date 63013: Day 4 without a credit card: Rain today with same predicted all week. Rain during a beach vacation means shopping, but unless there's a dollar store in the vicinity, shopping opportunities are limited. Check the FedEx tracker for card's whereabouts. It's hung up in Rocky Mount, NC, reason unclear. Consider the bigger picture and check the Wall Street Journal to see if the effect on the economy has registered. Nothing yet. Stay strong America. Stay strong.

Winter's Log, Star Date 70113: Day 5 without a credit card: The feeling of being out of step with the world intensifies. Learn credit card is still in Rocky Mount; scour the Internet for jobs as it appears I must move there. Briefly uplifted when FedEx truck is spotted, but spirits fall when attempt to wave it down fails. Nearly hyperventilate when hotel staff sheepishly admits they forgot to go to the post office. At 4 p.m., I'm alerted the card has arrived and hightail it to the lobby before something else can happen. Clutching card tightly, I notice the message printed on the envelope: "Guaranteed to arrive before the end of the day." Based on this inability to count or tell time, I wonder if card balance was cancelled along with previous card. No matter, I'm back, baby!

Elizabeth A. Winter-Sharpe

No Autographs, Please

A few years ago, my friend Elsi and I went to New York City for a long weekend of fun. Elsi had been many times and was a wonderful guide who indulged me with the "tourist experience."

We went to Times Square, Rockefeller Center (including an opportunity to watch a run-through of Seth Myer's monologue), Junior's Deli, the New York Public Library, Macy's (because I wanted to see an A-level store,) Ellen's Stardust Diner, and the Soup Kitchen International where I bought soup and interacted with the man after whom Seinfeld's "Soup Nazi" was modeled. We also went to two Broadway shows – *Jersey Boys* and *Kinky Boots*.

Jersey Boys was my first Broadway show and it was so good it was all I could do to not rush the stage and sing along. We met the cast afterwards, collecting autographs and gushing over them.

The next day, sitting in the lovely Al Hirschfeld Theatre waiting for *Kinky Boots* to begin, we were witness to an elderly couple sitting behind us. It appeared English was their second language and one was trying to explain the meaning of the word, "kinky," to the other. No matter the language, confusing explanations seem to happen the same: say it once, say it again only louder, say it a third time punctuating each word with a period. Hilarious.

Kinky Boots was wonderful. Billy Porter was amazing; I was entranced. Afterwards, we waited at the stage entrance with about 100 other people to meet the cast. I simply had to meet Billy Porter and thank him for his incredible performance. Perhaps, get his autograph; probably become fast friends. You know, the usual.

Sawhorses were set up outside the stage door, creating an aisle for the performers to walk through without a crush of people impeding them. Evidently, when the sawhorses end, the performers are on their own. We stationed ourselves about halfway down the length of the sawhorses and waited patiently.

We met Charlie and Don and Pat and Nicola. We met Trish, Lauren, and The Angels. I think we met the orchestra, the stagehands and the ticket takers. But no Lola. About half the crowd remained.

My eyes on the stage door, I willed Billy to come through it. Had he snuck out? Was he waiting us out? Could it be old and bothersome to have adoring fans? Did he know *I* was waiting, his new friend-to-be?

At long last, the door opened and there he was. I watched as he made his way through the sawhorses, speaking kindly to people without slowing his momentum. He didn't sign any autographs.

When he got to me, I said, "Thank you for a wonderful performance! I loved the show. Are you willing to autograph my program?"

He responded, "Yes, just a moment, please."

He took a few more steps towards the sawhorse exit, motioned forward, and said, "OK, everyone come here."

I thought he was talking to those who had asked for an autograph. So, I caught up and walked in lockstep with him, coming together when he exited the sawhorse aisle.

He then said, "OK, everyone, gather together. Those in front, crouch down."

Elizabeth A. Winter-Sharpe

Thinking this was some unusual, pre-autograph ritual, I did as directed and crouched down next to Billy Porter. Only then did I notice the photographer, standing in front of a school bus. The school bus that brought a group of high school students to see *Kinky Boots*. The group of high school students who were lucky enough to have their photo taken with Broadway star, Billy Porter. And me.

I can only imagine the conversations back at the school as they tried to figure out the identity of the strange woman in the photo.

Here's a lesson for all you kids out there: For an impressive photo bomb, be in the front row and be with Billy Porter.

High Maintenance Décor

I bought a 9-inch-tall rock formation of amethyst (called a "cathedral") because I love stone, amethysts and purple. It came with very specific directions to prepare it before it was to be displayed:

- Wash it in cold running water. Dry it by dabbing gently with soft cotton cloth.
- Wait one hour after sunset of the next new moon and put it outside where it will be exposed to cool air, wind, the moon and stars.
- Bring it indoors at 9:00 a.m. the next morning and place it in the sun for one hour.
- Rinse it in cool running water. Dab dry again.
- Smudge around it with sage or incense and then place it on a candle-lit home altar for 6-9 hours.
- Bury it in earth or sea salt for at least three days.

I modified the instructions slightly:

- Open box.
- Put amethyst on sofa table.
- Throw box in recycling bin.

Elizabeth A. Winter-Sharpe

Open Door Policy

It started with a photo album, or really, the making of one. At the time, it was popular to take a perfectly serviceable photo album and cover it with hot glue, batting, the fabric of your choice, and copious amounts of lace. You did this, of course, so your photo album reflected your fabulous taste and personality, and drew attention away from the blurry, badly-lit photos of red-eyed, semi-headless people that graced your album.

I craft on occasion because there's a crafter in me dying to burst free and create. However, let her loose and she'll paint, decoupage, sew, knit and bedazzle truly awful "art" because she doesn't have a lick of artistic talent.

The photo album, though, seemed possible. It didn't appear to require talent and the measurements could be guesstimates. And I'd get to use hot glue. From a gun.

I lived in an old house that had been converted into three apartments. My spare bedroom was now the designated craft room but I needed a table, preferably an old one I couldn't ruin. (I'd never completed a project without my clothes, hair, the walls, furniture or floor being covered in the medium of the day whether it be paint, glue, glitter, clay or wax.)

I asked my landlord, an aging hippie who meant well but wasn't the brightest light on the marquee, to keep an eye out for an old table. He replied, "No sweat. I'll make you one from stuff I already have."

I got home the next day and found my landlord standing at my side door, beaming. "Prepare yourself," he said, "I just installed your table." I remember wondering what he meant by "installed."

He opened the door to the spare room with a flourish, exclaiming, "Voila!," and there, suspended from brackets bolted to the wall was my new table. It was over six feet wide, about three feet deep and two inches thick with a smooth, brown laminate top. Curiously, near the table's front edge and about midway across the table was a hole, about three inches in diameter. He proudly exclaimed, "That's for your coffee cup. It's my own design."

Though not what I expected, I thanked him profusely and promised him a photo album. As I walked him out, I glanced towards the living room and stopped dead in my tracks. My front door was gone!

"Oh my God! My door's gone! Someone stole my door!" Wait. Who steals a door?

"It's copasetic, mama," he said, "I used the door to make your table."

He smiled proudly at his ingenuity and I asked, "Copasetic? Mama? What about my door? I *need* a front door."

He pondered this for a moment, his expression puzzled, and slowly the problem dawned on him.

"Ah," he said, "Bummer. Well, I have another door in the basement. You can have that one."

I didn't ask the obvious questions – like why he didn't use the spare door for the table and exactly what drugs he took in the 60's – but waited for him to install my "new" front door.

He did so in fairly short order and exclaimed, "Problem solved!"

Well, sort of.

The new door was a full six inches shorter than the door frame. Why? He had cut off the bottom of the door and affixed it to the wall under my new craft table to serve as support.

Elizabeth A. Winter-Sharpe

Picturing every rabbit, raccoon, squirrel, cat and small dog (and a few unsavory creatures) that now had unimpeded access to my living room, I pointed out this new wrinkle.

"I hear you," he said, nodding, "Got it covered." He proceeded to nail several pieces of scrap wood perpendicular to the bottom of the front door and edged them with weather-stripping.

He was clearly pleased with himself and I realized I was not the only craft-impaired person. How could I complain? It was art, after all, of his own design.

Communication Woes, Handyman Hoes

As most married people would tell you, there are times when you must walk a tightrope worthy of Barnum & Bailey. Sometimes, the tightrope is so harrowing, the Ringling brothers would be impressed, too.

In my first marriage, one tightrope involved me trying to *prevent* my (now) ex-husband from doing home maintenance.

Ex worked hard keeping the yard tidy and the cars pristine, but home maintenance was not his strong suit.

As an example, he loved to paint interiors but he couldn't see shades well, even with glasses. As a result, any given wall would have several ragged stripes of subtly different colors, caused by varying numbers of coats being applied in different sections of the wall. I would have happily called it a purposeful fashion statement if the only the stripes were remotely straight or even going in the same direction.

Ex was a firm believer in using toothpaste to fill holes in the wall. It was actually a good idea because he didn't believe in using tape measures or levels so our house smelled minty fresh due to the sheer number of holes in the walls.

I didn't want to criticize – he was trying to do the work – but I also didn't want to live in a patchwork quilt of a house.

My parents had a handyman, Jesse, who did all their odd jobs. He worked for all their friends, too, and the senior circle thought he did a good job for a reasonable price. Plus, he loved to talk, which they thought a bonus.

Elizabeth A. Winter-Sharpe

When I finally broached the subject of hiring a handyman, I told Ex, "We both have jobs. We both work hard. Plus you do all the yard work and maintain the cars, why don't we just hire Jesse for the occasional odd job and take the heat off of you?"

He didn't like the idea but did like the appeal to his vanity, so he begrudgingly agreed even as he predicted trouble. "What if something goes wrong? What are you going to do then?" Looking back, I thought he was referring to the handyman making a mistake.

We hired Jesse and he did a variety of projects for us – replacing the hot water heater, changing out light fixtures and the like. Ex came to like Jesse because they were both talkers and a 30-minute job would turn into two hours of "man chat."

One day, Jesse was scheduled to replace our front window with a bay window. Ex and I had to work and since Jesse couldn't be there until about 10, we just left the key under the mat for him.

Shortly after I got to work, my back went out. Luckily, I worked in the same building as my doctor and was able to see her before she started her regular office hours. She gave me a prescription and sent me home to lie down.

I decided I'd better leave a note for Jesse so that he would know I was home and wouldn't be startled. I reasoned he'd probably unload his supplies and equipment in front of the window before entering the house. So, to be sure he'd see it, I took a big piece of wrapping paper, wrote the note on the back and taped it to the front window, facing the street.

A short while later, Ex called me and said, "What are you doing?"

I said, "What do you mean? I left you a message. My back went out so I came home."

He said, "No. Jesse just called me. He's afraid to come in the house. He said you propositioned him."

Tales of the Terminally Awkward

I said, "I most certainly did not! I haven't even seen him! I left him a note so he'd know I was here."

"Yeah. What did the note say?"

It said, "Jesse: I want you to know I'm in the bedroom. Come on in. Ex is at work."

Oh. Alright. I can see how that's a little awkward.

Unfortunate that it was taped to the front window, too.

So, we had to get a new handyman. And move.

Elizabeth A. Winter-Sharpe

Finishing Touch

My (now) ex-husband worked for an asbestos abatement company. As a result he often came home with trinkets he found inside walls or hidden in the ceiling joists. The shelves in the garage were a shrine to forgotten lives: a well-used thermos, a plaque honoring a salesman of the quarter in 1972, and a framed photograph of what appeared to be construction workers in the 30s. (No, I don't know why he felt the need to bring these items home or keep them. Pick your battles.)

One day he came home almost giddy, having found a pair of handcuffs. Such devices were not part of our lifestyle, but we had a good chuckle.

To extend the joke, I hung the handcuffs on one of the (very tall) posts of our four-poster bed, where they faded into the background as most accessories do.

Around the same time, we were redoing the master bedroom. We had just gotten new carpet and painted the walls. I had a quilt made for our bed. Called "Stained Glass," it had a black background with starbursts of bright blues, pinks and purples. It was beautiful.

I've never been artistically talented but decided to try my hand at the finishing touch: I painted a black border around the top of the white walls and created a stencil that matched the pattern in our quilt. I stenciled the pattern using the same colors in the quilt, including the white "stitches." I thought it turned out pretty well and turned my attention to the bedside table, which had a tightly woven wicker inlay with a glass top. I removed the glass and painted the wicker with the same stencil design, then replaced the glass top. The room was lovely, if I do say so myself.

A few weeks later, we had my parents over for dinner. While the men were fixing drinks, my mom asked to see the bedroom she'd heard so much about. I happily led her down the hall and no sooner flipped on the light when I noticed the forgotten handcuffs hanging from the post at the head of the bed. For some reason, they now sparkled in the light, daring you to ignore them. My mouth dropped open and, thankfully, my brain kicked into gear.

Desperately trying to get her to focus downward, I screeched, "LOOK at the carpet," pointing at the nice but nondescript light gray carpet.

"Isn't it pretty? It's soft, too, you should take your shoes off to feel it!" "Go ahead! TAKE OFF YOUR SHOES!"

Ignoring me completely, my mother was running her hands over the quilt.

"Ooooh, it's beautiful," she gushed, "You're so talented!"

"Thanks, Mom, but I didn't make the quilt. Remember? Ok, we'd better get back to the kitchen."

"Oh, they'll be fine. I want to take a closer look at the border and the table."

I took her arm and walked her to the table, pointing at it to focus her attention downward. "I think I made a mistake, Mom. See if you can find it! (I knew this activity would keep her attention.)

After examining the table and pointing out mistakes I hadn't noticed," she said, "Now, let's see that border . . . "

"MOM! Look at it over there where the light is better," I said, steering her to the opposite corner of the bedroom.

Finally, I could take it no more and told her we had to return to the kitchen.

She didn't seem to notice my agitation and chattered on about my beautiful work.

Elizabeth A. Winter-Sharpe

"Honey!" she said to my dad, "Go look at their bedroom. You won't believe it unless you see it yourself!

Dutifully, I took him to the bedroom and followed the same, albeit abbreviated, routine: gushed about the carpet, motioned vaguely to the table and pointed to the border in the opposite corner of the room from the offending bedpost. I quickly ushered him out of the room and back to the kitchen where Mom was waiting.

"Well? What do you think? I want to try the same thing in our bedroom! Would you like it? I think it would be great!"

Mom trailed off, distracted by the cat who thankfully chose that moment to bless us with his presence.

My dad looked at me and quietly said, "I'd answer her but I'm not sure if she's talking about the wall border or the handcuffs!"

I stared at him in amazement and it occurred to me I wasn't so sure either.

Fifty Shades of Winter

Curiosity got the best of me. With all the hype around the *Fifty Shades of Grey* trilogy, I decided to read it but I didn't want witnesses. In other words, I couldn't buy it at a bookstore and I certainly couldn't borrow it from the library. I know people at the library.

Then it hit me. Nook. I could buy the book from Barnes and Noble. It would be downloaded directly to my iPad and I'd never have to interact with another person. There'd be no snarky comments, no rolling of the eyes, no judgmental looks, real or imagined, about my reading choices.

So, I read the book. Meh. Like any "romance" novel I've ever read, it was full of implausible situations and problems blown out of proportion, most of which could be solved by someone asking a simple question. The hero was perfect, save one *major* flaw. The heroine was, for lack of a better word, simple, even though she was described as merely naive.

As for the S&M (a dominant theme or a SUBtext, puns intended) I liked the popular MEME that stated Fifty Shades was only "romantic" because he was a billionaire; if he were poor, he'd be a criminal.

After the book hype died down, it wasn't long before the movie hype began. Once again, I felt compelled to see it - close the loop and all - but didn't know how to do it. I would never see it in public. I couldn't buy it in a store, didn't want it listed on my cable bill, nor did I want it listed in my Amazon purchases or stored on my Nook. Having the book was bad enough.

Elizabeth A. Winter-Sharpe

A friend of mine was teasing me. "You can buy it at Walmart. Who's going to judge you there? Just buy it." These texts were interspersed with photos of the store display and "thumbs up" emoji.

The next day I found myself at Walmart. For something else entirely, I swear.

I walked past the display and slowed my pace. My inner monologue began to argue...with itself.

"Look, it's on sale."

"I don't care."

"That's a good price."

"I'm not buying it."

"Why not? Just get it. You know you want to."

"Absolutely not! What if someone sees me?"

"Who's going to see you? You can go through the self-checkout then no one will see!"

"Oooooh. The self-checkout...I never thought of that. Good idea. OK, I'll do it!"

I picked up the DVD and hid it beneath my purse on the child seat of my shopping cart. I picked up a few other items - grocery camouflage - and headed for the self-checkout.

It was busy, but I smiled when I saw there was one register free and made a beeline for it.

I was cool, no reason to be embarrassed, I told myself. I scanned a grocery item and put it in the bag. I scanned another. Then I unearthed the DVD. Without hesitation, I slid it across the scanner. An alarm assaulted my ears and a red light flashed over my head, signaling the cashier that a customer needed assistance and notifying all those within a 30-yard radius that this customer was buying something inappropriate.

In no hurry to quell the casino-like lights and sounds emanating from the register, the cashier lumbered over to address the problem.

Conspiratorially, I leaned in and whispered, "I tried to scan the DVD."

"WHAT?"

"I just tried to scan the DVD."

"WHAT DVD? OH, YOU'RE TRYING TO BUY THAT FIFTY SHADES MOVIE? WE HAVE TO PUT IN YOUR BIRTHDATE. I CAN SEE YOU'RE OLD ENOUGH."

Another clerk called out, "DO YOU NEED ME?"

"NO! SHE'S JUST BUYING THAT FIFTY SHADES MOVIE" as she held the DVD over her head to show the curious onlookers. "We been sellin' a bunch of these - all types buying it. You musta liked the book."

Now fifty shades of purple, I mumbled that it's a gift for a friend, which is met with a sly chuckle. "Sure it is, honey. It's Christmas in July. Now what's your birthdate?"

I sheepishly left the store, not looking at anyone in case they knew the contents of my shopping bag. Home, I poured a drink and watched the movie. Wow. I thought just purchasing it was punishment.

Elizabeth A. Winter-Sharpe

Social Distancing Log

Social Distancing Eve: Prepare my half of the study to begin working from home tomorrow. Gather task list and files from tote bag, sort all files according to scheduled use. Place files on desk within easy reach of my computer, mouse, message pad, pen and coaster.

Realize a few more things are needed to really make it an office. Add scissors, a stapler, tape and a second coaster. Run to the store to get paper clips, a staple remover and tape dispenser. Oooh, they have metallic paperclips. And a purple pencil sharpener! I'd better get a pencil, too.

Arrange desk with new items. See desk is too crowded to work and put everything in drawer. Desk looks empty; fan out files. Make artful arrangement with phone, lotion and chapstick. Bring plant from other room.

Decide to add candy bowl to make it homey. Run to store to get candy. Can't decide; buy three different kinds, all chocolate. It's not like I'm taking meetings.

Desk is perfect! I should have cleaned it first. Remove everything, clean desk. Start over. Can't remember how it was all arranged. Put candy bowl next to computer and leave it at that.

Day 1: Late to work today. Traffic. From the bedroom to the study. Can't find my glasses either. Blaming cats for both. Wasn't there more candy in that bowl? I'll think about it over a Peppermint Patty. It seems breakfast-y somehow.

Good, solid day of work. I'm all in. Wait. It's 9:15 a.m.

Tales of the Terminally Awkward

Work steadily through the day: writing, planning, fielding calls, solving problems, plowing through emails. At 4:42 p.m. I have a sudden realization – my face just hit my desk. I dozed off. From this angle, I spy my lost glasses.

Day 2: Off to a strong start! On time, rested and rarin' to go. Hmmm, I never noticed that spot on the ceiling before. More of a shadow really. Or is it? Change angles. Spot still there. Change lighting. Spot still there. My office-mate, Hubs, is unconcerned. When prodded, he looks and says, "It's just a shadow."

Try to climb onto desk using desk chair. It does not go well as chair is on wheels. Put ice bag on my elbow and recall my mother telling me – frequently – I was smarter than this.

Get chair from kitchen. Cats gather for the show. Hubs shakes head and sighs heavily. Use stationary chair to climb onto desk. Wait. Need a flashlight. Climb down and go find flashlight. Back on chair, climb onto desk. Oops. Should have tested flashlight first. Climb down. Look for batteries. Back on chair, climb onto desk.

Huh. Just a shadow.

Day 3: Woke up with a brilliant plan for a new project I've been assigned. I just need a few hours without distraction to get it down on paper.

Hubs has been working the phone to schedule a root canal. Leaves whistling. Strange. Yet perfect.

Turn off phone. Turn off email notifications. Cats sleeping off early morning catnip treat. Ready. Set. Aah! Someone rang the doorbell! Who is it? How do they know I'm home? Oh. Right.

But I'm not expecting anyone. This is how every episode of *Criminal Minds* starts! Murderers are a wily bunch.

AAH! They rang it again! Clearly, a persistent murderer who won't give up until he (or she) kills me.

The cats are hiding. They're supposed to have a sixth sense about this stuff, right?

Stealthily, I creep to the study doorway and peek out towards the front window.

I'm shocked when I lock eyes with . . . the mail carrier, holding the package I ordered. Oh. Hey.

Day 4: Getting into the rhythm of working from home. Less distracted. Did Hubs' chair always squeak like that?

Planning a major event. Much easier to do without distractions. Wait. An email chime. It's my boss, scheduling a "Google Hangout." I snicker at the thought. On a conference call, no one will be the wiser that I haven't showered, dressed, put on makeup or combed my hair, which today resembles sort of a lazy Mohawk. Oh. I just noticed the swath of strawberry jam on my pajama top. Still, no one is the wiser.

I call the number and settle in. My boss, says "This is a video conference. Turn your camera on." What?

Day 5: Up early. Showered, dressed, made-up and coiffed. Heck, spritz of perfume - Smell-a-Vision can't be far off.

Repair to office and notice a faint path in the carpet between my desk and the kitchen. Go to kitchen to see if it's visible from there, too. Most definitely.

Vow to quit snacking between meals. Snort. Giggle. Full on laugh out loud. Who would have expected the expression "forge a new path" could be referencing the study to the kitchen?

So glad tomorrow is the weekend. Looking forward to...Oh, right. Staying home.

Look Out World

Many years ago I had a fellowship working in the press office of Ohio Senator John Glenn. For six months, I lived on Capitol Hill and enjoyed every minute of living and working in D.C. I have gone back many times over the years and one trip stands out in my memory.

I was visiting two friends and we went to one of my favorite spots – Mr. Smith's in Georgetown. Mr. Smith's served wonderful strawberry daiquiris but, let's be honest, we mainly went because the Navy boys from Bethesda often went there to sing along at the piano bar.

This particular night my friends and I were walking down K Street; I was busy talking to them and not looking where I was going. Unfortunately, I walked straight into a man who had just exited a cab. I apologized profusely, more so when I noticed his white cane. As it happens, he also was the piano player at Mr. Smith's. He was very kind and accepted my apology.

Once inside, my friends and I went downstairs to have drinks and catch up. Another friend wanted to meet up with us so I excused myself to call him and let him know where we were. Just as I hung up the phone, I turned and ran smack into the piano player. Again! I apologized repeatedly and, once again, he very kindly accepted my apology.

A couple hours and a few drinks later, I went upstairs to use the restroom. As I was leaving, you guessed it, I ran into the piano player a third time. This time, he took my hands and said, "Honey, are you blind, too?"

Elizabeth A. Winter-Sharpe

Just a Gigolo

There comes a time when we have to recognize who we are as an individual, own our flaws and take at least some responsibility for situations we find ourselves in. Consider this my moment.

A few years ago, I went to a conference in Orlando, Florida. The resort was incredible. It had every service and amenity you could imagine – multiple restaurants, bars, shops, spa services, etc. And it was gorgeous.

When I got to my room I noticed that there were lights affixed to the wall on either side of the bed, and one was hanging askew. It looked like it was just missing a screw so I made a mental note to report it in the morning.

When I left my room the next day, a housekeeper was in the hall. I didn't want her to think it was a big problem, so I said, "Excuse me, I have a problem and I'm hoping you will help me. The light in my room is broken. I think a screw will take care of it. Can you help me with that?"

Based on her accent, I surmised English was her second language and I tried to be sensitive to that because she said to me, "You need a screw?"

Thinking she intended for me to fix it, I thought, "Sure, why not," and answered, "Yes, I need a screw."

Then she said, "You want I get man for you?"

Thinking she was referring to the maintenance man, I said, "Yes, thank you! It would be great if you could get a man for me! I'd be very happy! Just so you know, I won't be back to my room until around six."

Curiously, she winked at me and said, "I get man with screw for you."

I replied, "Excellent. Thank you! I will look forward to tonight!" (I like to read in bed.)

When I arrived to my floor, I was surprised to see the housekeeper still in the hall. She smiled at me and said, "I get man with screw for you!"

I smiled and said, "Thank you! I've been looking forward to this evening!"

I opened the door to my room and the first thing I noticed – different than when I left – was the armoire. The shelf was now extended and held an ice bucket, a bottle of wine, two wine glasses and a rose.

Before I could process this, from the other side of my room stepped a man! He gave me a big smile, opened his arms and said, "Hello. I am here with screw for you!"

It was at this point I started to do the math and thought, "Oh my God, did she get me a gigolo?"

My next thought was, "Wow! This IS a full service hotel."

Then I thought, "Do I have to tip them both?" Because I don't know the protocol.

He and I looked at each other for a long minute and I got nervous. Sadly, when I get nervous, I get awkward and start babbling, usually nonsense. To this man I said:

"I am so sorry, I'm married. Well, I'm not sorry I'm married. Well, sometimes I'm sorry I'm married but…you know how that is. Maybe you don't. I'm not prying. It's just that I can't do this because I'm married. If I weren't married…well, I still couldn't do this because I'm just not that kind of person. No judgment. I'm sure you're very good at your… craft. I'm just saying I can't do this. I'm married. But thank you. I appreciate the effort. And good luck."

He looked at me, seemingly puzzled, put his hand in his pocket and pulled out a screw. He said, "Ma'am, I have screw for you."

Now I was nervous *and* embarrassed and somewhat confused. He was not wearing a uniform of any sort. So I said, "Well...good. Here's the thing. I have to go. You can go ahead and do what you have to do, just without me being here. That's ok. Right? So, thank you and good night." I ran out of my room and sprinted down the hall.

The housekeeper – still in the hall – looked puzzled. I grabbed $20 out of my purse and handed it to her saying, "Split this between you and the man. I have to go!"

I went to a bar downstairs. I sat there for two hours just to be sure he had time to clear out.

Looking back, I'm still not sure what happened but I admit I may have played a part in causing it. So, let's just turn this into a piece of advice: Be careful what you ask for because you might just get a gigolo!

How Now Brown Cow

Having traveled a fair bit, I've found it interesting (and appalling) to learn the reputation Americans often have in other countries. It generally hovers between us being selfish, spoiled brats and rude, arrogant know-it-alls. I'm hyper-aware when I'm a guest in another country and try my best to counteract these perceptions. On the other hand, I've witnessed the behavior of some of my compatriots – they're not helping matters.

What's interesting is the stereotypes we have about each other. I bet you can come up with a few by state, e.g. New Yorkers are rude, Californians are hippy-dippy – and those are some of the kinder examples.

I experienced this myself a few years back when I went to New York City on a business trip. Since I had a free afternoon, I decided to splurge with a visit to the salon of a hair stylist who was famous for being part of a reality TV show. I wanted said stylist to cut my hair, but at $500 a pop, I was content to watch him wield his scissors from afar.

He seemed nice, stopping twice to let a salon customer take his photo. Meanwhile, his own customer was reading a magazine, steadfastly ignoring him. I found this to be a rather obvious violation of the stylist/stylee code, which requires the dishing of juicy gossip and the sharing of secrets. Even if he wasn't telling tales about his celebrity colleagues, it became clear why he was so expensive. He literally had a helper standing next to him who held out each lock of hair for the stylist to snip.

Elizabeth A. Winter-Sharpe

Though I wouldn't shell out $500 for a cut, I did choose to see a "master stylist" named Arizona for $130. He was a very nice man who declared my current hairstyle "boring" and insisted I needed an "edgy new coif." I decided to be brave and headed off to the shampoo chair with his young assistant, Kimmy.

Kimmy was polite and we had the obligatory weather conversation. She noted my "accent" and asked where I was from originally. I told her I was from Ohio and only in New York for business.

"OHIO! Really?" she squealed. "I've never met anyone from Ohio! What kind of cow do you have?"

Puzzled, I asked, "Cow?"

"Of course. Everyone in Ohio is a farmer and all farmers have a cow," she said with certainty and some suspicion since I didn't seem to know this about the state I call home.

Like a shopping mall Santa, as her first Ohioan, I felt a certain responsibility to fulfill the illusion. "Oh, you said COW. Absolutely," I declared. "It's the law that we all have to have at least one cow."

"Wow!" she breathed, her beliefs confirmed, "The law."

Now feeling a little out of place at the pricey salon, I looked from side to side, as if making sure no one was listening and whispered, "Don't tell anyone, but I have five cows."

In awe, she whispered, "Whoa. Five?! I promise I won't tell anyone!"

Kimmy escorted me back to Arizona's station and stood by his side. Apparently, none of these folks can work alone. Like a surgical tech, Kimmy handed him each implement upon command.

"Comb!" She smacked the comb into his hand.

"Scissors." Smack.

Tales of the Terminally Awkward

"Blow dryer." Smack.

She smiled at me in the mirror the entire time, apparently thrilled to be my confidant.

While he worked, Arizona entertained me with stories about the reality show celebrities that frequented the salon. He was so engaging, I didn't notice what he was doing to my head. Ultimately, my "edgy" new style was a short, spiked mullet – think Joan Jett in the early years. Sadly, I was a 48-year-old would-be Ohio farmer turned businessperson.

Proclaiming my new style, "kicky," Kimmy escorted me to the door, wished me safe travels back to the farm, and asked that I say "hello" to the cows for her.

All I could say was, "I bet the cows will act like they've never seen me before."

Elizabeth A. Winter-Sharpe

Flying Solo

I was an apple in a world of pears, well, pairs. It had been a rough few months and I needed a break. I chose to take a short cruise so that I could relax in the sun, have a few drinks, read a couple of books, casually chat with other vacationers.

I wasn't ready for the utter disbelief when my fellow passengers learned I was traveling alone. I wasn't ready for the shocked silence, the exchanged looks, the search for something to say. I wasn't ready for the too big smiles that accompanied, "Good for you!"

Day one was spent traveling and unpacking. I was exhausted and opted not to go to the dining room for dinner as it's usually a somewhat lengthy affair. Alright, I was also a little apprehensive. Instead, I chose to go to a specialty restaurant, a hamburger joint set up like a 50's diner. In addition to the paper hats and the tabletop jukeboxes, the staff also had attitudes from the 50's.

The host greeted me warmly with a big smile. When asked "How many," I replied "One" and the confusion began. He picked up two menus and looked hopefully behind me. "One," I repeated. He looked confused and turned back to look into the nearly empty restaurant. Rather than escort me to a table, he handed me a menu and said, "Sit anywhere."

Ensconced in a booth, I felt I had navigated the worst and it wasn't so bad. One menu, one person, the math is clear.

The server came to the table and introduced himself. From Romania, Victor greeted me kindly and asked if my husband would be joining me.

"No, just me."

"Who is joining you?"

"No one. It's just me."

"You're here alone?"

"Yes."

"You are on the cruise alone?"

"Yes."

A long silence ensued. His face went from puzzled to disbelief to forced happiness. "That is good?" he asked hopefully.

"Absolutely."

Eating my feelings, I ordered a burger, fries and a chocolate milkshake. He brought me the milkshake with the straw wrapper folded into an origami heart. He then returned behind the counter where he and two of his co-workers watched me in silence. I'd forgotten to bring a book so I had nothing to distract me from being watched like a zoo animal. With regards to Noah, the one animal without a partner.

The next day I decided to look for someone (anyone) else who may be alone - perhaps we could join forces for a show or a meal. At a cocktail party that evening, I noticed a man of about 45, seated alone. Ordinarily, I wouldn't automatically conclude he was traveling alone but he was wearing the LOUDEST royal blue plaid jacket I had ever seen and his ill-fitting green-striped shirt was topped with a floral bow tie. There was no way a spouse, girlfriend or partner would let him out in that ensemble.

The captain spoke a few minutes later and introduced those in attendance who had been the most faithful to the cruise line. The man in question was introduced and I learned he was traveling with his mother who happened to be ill that evening.

I also met two women whom I affectionately call the Lush sisters. They arrived late to the cocktail party and were already six sheets to the wind. For some reason, they glommed onto me.

The most talkative of the two asked if the captain had spoken yet. Learning she had missed it, she expressed her disappointment and asked if I knew if he were the same captain that she'd met seven years before. I told her "No, it couldn't be," because it was his first day sailing.

Clearly too drunk to realize my answer was both improbable and utterly ridiculous, she became worried and repeated my comment - and her concern - to her companion.

"It's his first day! That doesn't seem safe. This boat is so big, it has to be hard to drive."

She looked around for someone official so she could express her concern. I told her not to worry. "Sailing is in his blood. His dad ran the glass-bottom boat tour in Nassau for years!"

"Whew!" she said, "So, he IS qualified. That's a relief."

I gently remind them that the cocktail party is almost over so if they want another free drink they'd better go get it. They take off after a waiter and I'm able to slip out.

Alone again. Happily.

Midwest Girls

At 50 years old and newly divorced, I had to figure out what to do about travel. It's my passion, but I didn't know anyone who was single, solvent and with similar interests. I had to get comfortable traveling by myself. Staying home was not an option.

As a trial trip, I chose a short Bahamian cruise. I had taken the trip before so I knew the boat, I knew the itinerary, I knew the ports, all of which would help me ease into my solo traveling status.

There were a couple of bumps the first few days but by day three I had adjusted and was looking forward to visiting Key West the next day. I'd always enjoyed visiting Key West.

I disembarked around 10 a.m., wandered around town to shop and have lunch. Afterwards, I saw a cute little bar that opened onto Duval Street. It had thatch-roof detailing and advertised a signature Rum Runner that looked delightful. For the first time in my life, I went into a bar by myself, sat at the bar and had a drink.

A man around my age sat a couple chairs down from me. He raised his glass to me and we started to chat. From Australia, Jim was in the fifth week of a six-week "world tour." He'd been to France, Germany, England and Canada before the U.S. He had flown into Miami and drove down to Key West. He was leaving in the morning to go to Orlando and a few other stops in the southeast before heading home.

He worked for the Australian government, which had a very generous vacation plan. I don't remember the specifics, but was seriously considering a move when *Crocodile Dundee* walked into the bar.

Elizabeth A. Winter-Sharpe

His name was actually Steve but he embodied every characteristic of Dundee (especially the obnoxious ones,) including the quiet sidekick who sipped his beer until it was time for him to laugh loudly at something Steve said. And Steve had a lot to say.

As the only other people in the bar, Steve took it upon himself to "entertain" us. He told a lengthy story about the tourist trap up the street where you could have your photo taken holding a huge snake. According to Steve, he grabbed the snake by the tail, spun it in a circle over his head and let it go flying into a crowd of tourists.

"Not the first time my big snake made the sheilas scream!" Cue sidekick to laugh uproariously.

Steve yelled everything so he clearly had no way to modify the volume of his voice. He also lacked even a modicum of tact or polish.

"Hey, mate, ya gonna bang her?!" he yelled at Jim.

Just then, a woman entered the bar and joined Steve and his sidekick. Curiously attired, she was wearing a strapless sundress, a straw hat and sunglasses, and had a long knit scarf wrapped around her neck as if it were the dead of winter.

We soon learned that she was Steve's ex-wife. She lived in Key West, Steve (and sidekick) had come stateside to visit her. All three were very drunk but they began to entertain each other, allowing Jim and I to resume chatting.

A few minutes later I hear, "Hey! You! Are you from around here? Hey! HEY!"

I turned to see Mrs. Steve waving to me from the corner of bar, about four chairs away. Hoping she was talking to anyone else, I looked around, but we were still the only other people in the bar.

I tried to respond in a manner that was kind but not inviting more conversation, "No, just visiting."

Tales of the Terminally Awkward

"Are you two a couple?"

"No. We were just talking."

"You're cute together."

"OK."

"Where you from?"

<Sigh> "Ohio."

SCREECH! "OHIO! ME, TOO! I'm seriously from Ohio!"

Mrs. Steve ran around the bar and enveloped me in a bear hug. "You're my best friend! My very best friend!" she sobbed into my neck.

Her mood changed in flash and she said, "Oh! I have to show you something. Something I got in Ohio. I want to know what you think."

I couldn't imagine what it was but waited patiently, demonstrating signature Midwest good manners and tolerance.

Mrs. Steve handed me her sunglasses, then took off her straw hat and shoved it into my arms. She unwound the long green scarf from around her neck and handed that over as well. Finally, she took her big denim purse off her shoulder and shoved that into the pile of her things resting on my lap.

"Here. THIS is what I want to show you." She proceeded to yank down the top of her sundress to show me – show all of us – her breasts.

The bar was silent except for Mrs. Steve saying, "*These* are from Ohio! What do you think?"

Having no idea what to say in such a situation, I put her belongings on the bar, wished Jim safe travels, nodded to Mrs. Steve and left. I still wonder why she was wearing the scarf though. Try as you might, you cannot keep Midwest girls under wraps.

Elizabeth A. Winter-Sharpe

Wish You Were Here

I've often thought that vacationing is my one true skill. To be sure, I'm not one of those manic travelers that tries to cram in as much as possible. I'm also not one that floats through the experience with a backpack and an open train pass. I'm somewhere in the middle, doing copious research followed by making extensive spreadsheets, resulting in balanced, perfect vacations. For me. Usually.

It's when you add people into the mix that vacations get interesting. Whether traveling companions or strangers you encounter, I've found a good sense of humor will take you far. Pun intended.

After my divorce, I took my dream trip to Austria. I traveled alone but was not lonely; I met numerous people throughout my trip.

I arranged my trip to start in Vienna so I could attend a mass with a performance of the Vienna Boys Choir. It was a beautiful chapel and I had purchased a front row seat so I wouldn't miss a thing.

My seat neighbor arrived just after me. About ten years my senior, we nodded and smiled at each other, and I tentatively said, "Good morning." His eyes lit up. "American?" "Yes."

Phillip was from Loveland, Colorado, also traveling alone. When he learned I was from Akron, Ohio, this conversation ensued:

"Akron! I have friends in Akron!"

"How about that. Small world." (It must be obligatory to say this at least once on every trip.)

"Do you know Ann Richards?"

"The former governor of Texas?"

"No. Stan and Leslie's daughter. They live in Akron."

"No, sorry, I don't know her. Or them."

"Are you familiar with the University of Akron?"

"Actually, yes. I'm an alum and worked there, too."

"And you don't know Stan? He taught there."

"Sorry. It's fairly large and I rarely met others outside of my department."

"There was a fraternity house on campus that used to be an old barn. Which fraternity was it?"

"I'm sorry, I don't know. I wasn't in a fraternity or sorority."

"Hey, are you sure you're from Akron?"

Evidently, a la Hooterville, he thought I should have crossed paths with the entire extended Richards clan at Sam Drucker's General Store or during one of Akron's monthly hoedowns.

Thankfully, the mass began so our conversation ended. With apologies to Stan, Leslie and Ann, if you speak to Phillip, please give him my regards.

I also went to my first opera in Vienna. Actually, I chose an operetta, *The Merry Widow*, which was a comedy, thinking it might be better for a first timer. I enjoyed it and appreciated the English subtitles flashing on the screens mounted in the lovely, old theater.

I planned to catch a cab back to my hotel after the performance. As there was no line, I simply chose a cab and told the driver the name of my hotel and the street. Stupidly, I thought that would be enough to bridge any language gap. I was wrong.

Elizabeth A. Winter-Sharpe

He spoke English but didn't believe I did. He yelled, "I can't understand you because of your accent!" I tried on a few different accents to no avail. Finally, he threw a map to me so I could find the street for him. That settled him down enough to converse with me.

"Are you from Chicago?"

"No."

"New York?"

"No. I'm from Akron, Ohio."

"Ohio! I hear the worst people are from Ohio!"

"That's right, buddy, and I'm their leader!"

He didn't say another word. I tipped him though. I didn't mean to scare him.

Throughout my travels in Europe, I've noticed that bathrooms always involve stairs. You will always go up or down to a bathroom and you will most likely need cash to use it. In fact, at Westbahnhof (train station) in Vienna you're charged 0.50 Euro to use the bathroom BUT you get a coupon for a free cup of coffee. It's an interesting business model.

One of my favorite experiences happened in Salzburg. I was at a hotel in Altstadt (Old Town.) It was about 11:00 p.m. and I had just gone to bed. There was a knock on my door and a man yelled, "Come on! Hurry up, we have to go!" I opened the door to find a 20-something man standing there. He turned beet red and apologized, saying he had the wrong room.

The same thing happened the next night except, when I answered the door, it was a different 20-something man standing there, clad only his underwear. I wondered if it was an Austrian custom and would have researched it but, well, I had to go.

Stamp of Approval

When Billy Joel wrote the song, *Vienna Waits for You*, I bet he was trying to fly there from Cleveland. I have some personal experience traveling from Cleveland to Vienna that bears this out.

I decided to take my dream trip to Austria, starting in Vienna, working my way over to Salzburg, with excursions to little villages and hamlets along the way, and ending in Zurich, Switzerland, since I'd be in the neighborhood.

Rather than an organized tour, I planned everything myself, determined to do exactly what I wanted to do. Everything went so smoothly, it seemed fated to be. I had saved enough air miles to cover the flight. An unexpected tax return paid for my hotels and train tickets.

I only had to pay for food, events and shopping. I was able to score tickets for the opera and a mass with the Vienna Boys Choir. And, of course, the number one excursion on my list - The Sound of Music tour.

I was to leave Cleveland at 6:00 p.m. and head to Toronto. An hour and a half layover and I was Munich-bound with a one-hour layover before my final destination of Vienna.

Anxious that all go well, I arrived at the airport three hours early. I was happily surprised when I was sent through the "express" security line. (After having been searched, swabbed, scanned and felt up by countless TSA agents across this great country, perhaps they had finally realized I'm about as threatening as a Labrador retriever.)

I exchanged my money for Euros and proceeded to the assigned gate to wait.

Elizabeth A. Winter-Sharpe

I remember looking out to the tarmac, grateful that the bad weather had moved on and would not delay my departure. Not so fast!

It seemed our previous bad weather *would* delay our departure because it was moving to Toronto, preventing all flights from landing. In an interesting twist, international flights leaving Toronto would continue as scheduled because they have to pay a hefty fine if they do not arrive at their destinations on time. The upshot: by the time I arrived in Toronto, my flight to Munich would be long gone.

The gate attendant began looking for other options for me. His fingers pounded the keyboard for 10 minutes; he never uttered a word. Finally, he announced the best possible plan: "You go home. Come back in the morning for a 9 a.m. flight to Washington Dulles. Wait there until 5 p.m. then fly to Dallas/Ft. Worth, then to Brussels, to Prague and then to Vienna, arriving about 48 hours later than planned."

"OR," said the other ticket agent as she looked over his shoulder, "We could send her from Toronto to London and then to Vienna." She looked at me apologetically and said, "You'll arrive about three hours after you originally planned." Hmmmm, what to do, what to do? (Eye roll)

In Toronto, once beckoned to the Customs desk, I smiled and greeted the agent, and handed over my passport, ticket and itinerary.

I have to admit I've had some problems with these entrance exams in the past. I want to answer correctly but consider their questions unclear.

As an example, he asked, "Where are you going?" and I responded with a question: "Do you mean my immediate destination or my ultimate destination or everywhere during my entire trip?"

He glared at me and repeated his question, a tad harshly. Therefore, I told him everything I knew: "My itinerary shows I was to go to Munich and then to Vienna, but due to the weather, I've been rerouted from here to London and then to

Tales of the Terminally Awkward

Vienna, as you see on my tickets. I'm then traveling throughout Austria and will come home from Switzerland."

He said, "So, you're going to Vienna."

"At one point, yes."

"And you're going for...?"

"10 days."

"No! Business or pleasure?"

"I'm sorry. But that's a *why* question. *Why* am I going? I'm going for pleasure."

He was getting pissed and I was getting flustered. I swear I was just trying to answer correctly. His next, and last, question was my favorite: "How are you getting home from Europe?"

Mind you, he was holding my itinerary. We just had the entire travel plan discussion. I thought I'd sound like a smart ass if answered "flying." But what were my options? (I'm reminded of comedian, Steven Wright, who, when stopped at the Canadian border and asked, "Do you have any weapons?," he replied, "What do you need?") These are not funny people.

In the alternative, was he doing some secret agent work to suss out any dangerous intentions I might have? Labrador!

Finally, he tired of me, handed back my documents and waved me through.

I had a similar experience in London, but in Vienna I simply followed the crowd and strolled right out of the airport and got into a cab. I remember thinking, "Hmmm, too bad, I really wanted a Vienna stamp in my passport."

Ten days later, I found myself standing at the Customs desk in Zurich. "Ma'am," said the agent, "How did you get into Europe?" <sigh>

Elizabeth A. Winter-Sharpe

I responded, "I flew from Cleveland to Toronto to London to Vienna and then traveled to Zurich by train."

"Can you explain why you don't have stamps in your passport?"

Uh-oh. Sensing potential trouble, I remembered the saying "the best defense is a good offense" and said, "No, I was going to ask you."

"What?"

"I wanted a Vienna stamp in my passport but I didn't know where to get it. I would have loved one in Toronto or London but they didn't do it either. I just followed the crowd whenever I got off a plane and here we are."

He kindly chose not to make me an international scofflaw, merely saying, "I'll give you an exit stamp but plan extra time for problems because you don't have an entry stamp."

Indeed, I flew back through Toronto and was immediately flagged at Customs. I had the distinct honor of meeting with some folks privately to straighten everything out, including a very personal pat down. I thought of my special Canadian Customs friend the entire time. Touché, sir.

Be Still My Heart

I enjoy asking my husband questions about unlikely, hypothetical situations. Think Cosmo quiz questions. Most men typically hate them but mine is such a sweetheart he indulges me. This is one of my favorite conversations:

"Hypothetical question. We receive a letter from the state that says a glitch occurred and our marriage is invalid. What do we do?"

"We go right down to City Hall and get married," he replies.

He looks into my eyes and smiles, and I'm certain he's about to say something wonderfully romantic. Instead, he says, "And then I'll take you out for a sandwich."

Incredulous, I ask, "That's it?!"

Puzzled, he says, "We can get some chips, too."

I adore this man.

Elizabeth A. Winter-Sharpe

Rapper's Delight

Of all the people I'd like to meet, LeBron James is at the top of the list. I'm not a fan because of his basketball career, though, you know, bravo. I'm a fan because of his generosity to those in need and, most importantly, because he's a terrific role model. I simply want to thank him personally.

I figured I should have a good chance of meeting him since we're both from Akron. I still live in the area and he reportedly visits fairly often. But the closest I've ever gotten was at a local event. I was less than 20 yards from him but was "boxed out" (That's a basketball term. Booyah!) before I could get any closer.

Since he also works on several projects with both of my employers, one might think the odds of our crossing paths would be significantly improved. Goodness knows I can't walk two feet from my desk without running into yet another coworker who has met him. And, for heaven's sake, two of his best friends were students of mine! That should count for something.

A few years ago, I was convinced my time had come. I was meeting with the manager of an area car dealership, completing the paperwork to lease a car. It was my third lease with him so we've known each other for years.

He was expressing how happy I was going to be with my new car and I said, "The only thing that would make me happier is to meet LeBron James."

He replied, "I've met LeBron James! He's bought cars from us and I've delivered them to his house."

My mouth dropped open and I blurted out, "You have to take me with you next time. I will wear a dealership polo shirt. I promise I will be entirely appropriate. You HAVE to take me with you. I want it written in this contract!"

He chuckled and said, "Last time I was there, I met Jay-Z."

"Is that his car guy?" I asked.

"Seriously?" he asked, incredulous. "JAY-Z!"

"What? Is he their manny or something?"

"No! You know, Queen B..."

"I thought you said his name was Jay-Z."

Just then, my husband joined us. The manager said to him, "You have to help me out."

"Why? Are you talking sports with her?" He was worried I had expressed my theory about the NFL needing team moms.

The conversation was recounted and the hubs did a face palm. Looking pained, he said, "C'mon, dear. JAY-Z!"

"I heard you both. Saying it louder doesn't help. I still don't know who he is or his friend, Queen B."

"He's a famous rapper. Queen B is Beyonce'. They're married."

"Oh. I've heard of her. You know I only listen to talk radio," I explained, trying to save face.

And so ended what I considered to be a golden opportunity to meet LeBron.

On the way home, the hubs tried to console me. "It's ok, dear. You'll meet him someday. And don't worry about not knowing Jay-Z. You can't know everyone. But maybe don't tell the kids. That would be embarrassing."

Elizabeth A. Winter-Sharpe

I'm not sure who he thinks will be embarrassed but, since I've already outed myself here: Kids, I'm sorry. I am not as "down with it" as you think I am. Or, let's be honest, as I'd like to think you think I am.

If only I could do something to redeem myself in their eyes…like meet LeBron James!

With my sincere apologies to Mr. Z.

Fan Frenzy

Sometimes I think my life is a study in contradictions. I believe in obeying the law but often "right-size" the speed limit. I'm an introvert who loves public speaking. I enjoy sports but don't care who wins. In fact, to my husband's dismay, I cheer for everyone who makes a good play because I think it's important to recognize everyone's good work.

My husband is a die-hard football fan, Browns and Buckeyes all the way. He will watch as many games as is physically possible. I enjoy watching football but not watching ALL the football.

When we were dating, Jeff would patiently explain all the rules and nuances of football to help me better understand and appreciate the game. In turn, I would watch for news about our local teams to share and discuss with him. In one notable football fail, when I heard about an injured Browns player I made a point to remember it so that I could tell him about it. Evidently, I didn't remember well enough as it turned out Miles Davis didn't even play for the Browns.

Jeff would also kindly listen when I explained my theory of having a team mom.

Charles Barkley once said he was not a role model; he was a basketball player. The backstory makes that statement more palatable – he believes parents should be the ones influencing their kids. Agreed. However, kids looking elsewhere for heroes is as old as time. Since it takes fans to pay player salaries, I contend players *should* be role models and it should be part of their contract. I don't think it's too much to ask that they obey the law and demonstrate good sportsmanship. I really don't. A team mom would help facilitate this.

We watched a game (I don't remember which one and it doesn't matter) and a player made an illegal play that was clearly not accidental. His team lost 15 yards. I was appalled.

"Fifteen yards!? That's ridiculous. The other guy could have been really hurt. If I were the team mom, I would pull that young man right off the field. I'd tell him to sit on the bench and THINK about what he's done. He'll play again when *I say* he can play again and not a minute sooner! And I'd tell the coach I don't want to hear it. That was unacceptable behavior!"

Jeff thinks this is hilarious so long as I don't share it with others, particularly friends watching the game with him. Football fans are sensitive, I've learned.

Some other items I've learned are:

- Though intellectually you know the refs can't hear you yelling helpful instructions at the TV, a true fan will continue to try.
- No matter how comforting your voice, saying, "Remember, it's just a game," is not as helpful as you might expect.
- If you make plans having forgotten to check the football schedule, a true fan will get you a schedule to keep in your purse. (Thank you, honey.)
- Sometimes, the best way to watch football is from the other room while shopping for shoes online.
- This is regional: "Woof Woof" is reserved for the Browns and is not appropriate after the O-H...I-O thingy.

Speaking of...I once made a football faux pas that was so awful, so egregious, that Jeff returned to a restaurant to apologize on my behalf.

Tales of the Terminally Awkward

We were on vacation in the Outer Banks and tried a little family-owned restaurant for lunch. Jeff is an extrovert and got to talking with the owner, staff and other patrons, learning many were from Ohio.

As we stood at the door about to leave, Jeff's phone rang so he stepped outside. By way of goodbye, the good folks looked at me, smiling, and shouted, "O-H!"

I decided to REPRESENT, threw my arms up in the air and shouted, "O-I!" The room went silent. It was pitiful. Just PITIFUL. I *knew* that one.

I went straight to the bench to think about what I had done.

Elizabeth A. Winter-Sharpe

Purse-onal Foul

My husband loves football and is a Cleveland Brown's fan through and through. When he was given two tickets for their first home preseason game in 2019, it was like Christmas had come early and Santa himself had dropped by with the news.

I suggested he take one of the kids or a friend, as they will appreciate the game far more than I, but he really wanted me to go with him. It was a beautiful day, I had some cute new sandals, so why not?

I hadn't been to a Brown's game for about 30 years but had gone to several Indians games and one Cavs game recently. Silly me, I thought it would be a similar experience.

As I usually do before attending events with thousands of people, I changed from my regular purse and took just a few items in a crossbody bag that measured about 5x7 inches.

We left about two hours before the game for what should be a 45-minute run. The first inkling of trouble was when it took an hour just to drive the mile or so down 9th Street. Unlike when we attended the Indians' and Cavs' games, we had to park a country mile away and hoof it. I wouldn't have minded but my cute sandals were not on board with this plan.

We arrived at the stadium and waited in line but when we reached the entrance, the attendant told me that my purse was too big and I was not allowed to enter. A small card hung around his neck and he told me that no one would be admitted if their purse was bigger than the card. Not having done the (evidently) requisite research prior to attending the game, we were unaware of this rule.

Tales of the Terminally Awkward

We were instructed to walk to a tent on the lake-side of the stadium, where I could lock up my purse for $10. I tried to get Jeff to go to our seats without me and I'd come along when my purse was stowed. He refused.

We made the trek and got in a long line of about 50 people. When we finally reached the front of the line, I had taken everything out of my purse and put it in my pockets so I simply handed over my purse and my $10, and got a claim ticket. They tossed my purse in a plastic bin with dozens of others.

The most painful thing at this point, aside from my feet, was seeing Jeff's face each time we heard the crowd cheer and he wasn't there to witness it. He steadfastly refused to go in without me, his face getting longer with each score.

It is important to note that I am a rule-follower. It was my mistake for not knowing about the NFL rule. However, I do expect that the rules be enforced fairly. Instead…

We walked to the nearest entrance. Three women were ahead of us in line. Two of them had purses TWICE the size of mine. One of them had a purse that was nearly the size of a saddle bag. All three were waved right in.

Just as bad, once we got into the stadium, I saw the woman who had been directly in front of us at the "dangerous purse tent." In her left hand she was carrying a clear plastic bag with all the items that had been in her purse. In her right hand she was carrying her NOW EMPTY PURSE!

Because of all this, we missed all but the last two minutes of the first quarter. And Jeff missed all of Baker.

Finally arriving at our seats, I noticed a message under the end zone screen. It was a phone number and an invitation to text if you had an issue, so I did.

Elizabeth A. Winter-Sharpe

I told my story, reiterating that my problem was not the rule itself, but that it was selectively enforced. Their reply was that they were sorry but the NFL made the rule and it had been in place for five years.

As it didn't respond to my message, I suggested staff training might be in order and offered up the title of #sizeDOESmatter.

They did not respond, obviously entranced by my wit, but I have a piece of advice for the Browns: If the NFL is so lackadaisical about measurements, you may want to check the chains. Who knows, maybe you would have made the playoffs!

Mixed Marriage

A year or so after I extricated myself from my first marriage, I decided to date. I tried several dating sites over the next couple of years, including OurTime, on which I met Jeff. We married 16 months after we met - not a whirlwind courtship but long enough at our age.

We really only had one dilemma, which we expected to some degree but found it to be a far bigger challenge than we anticipated. You see, we are a mixed couple. When I say that, I mean he's a packrat and I'm a purger.

When we moved into our new home it became clear just how big of a problem we were facing.

A word of advice...if you ever find yourself combining two households, get your stuff there first. Otherwise - and I know from experience - your stuff may not fit!

Jeff does not mind me writing about this but he wants it to be clear that he is NOT a "hoarder." He simply loves a good sale and hates to throw anything away. Still, we had so much stuff that for two months we had to create paths in the house just to get around.

This is a partial inventory of what the love of my life brought to our new home:

- 17 rectangular Pyrex baking dishes
- Eight sets of eight glasses each
- FIVE crockpots
- Four HUGE boxes of spices, which included nine bottles of nutmeg, eight bottles of cinnamon, four large containers of Tony Chachere's Creole Seasoning and a whole bunch of spices that were older than me!

Elizabeth A. Winter-Sharpe

For the record, yes, he cooks but he is not A cook.

Moving away from the kitchen, he also came equipped with:

- 14 bottles of toilet bowl cleaner
- 27 rolls of paper towels
- 42 polo shirts
- 68 light bulbs. (Yes, I counted. Don't judge me.)

And, while I won't give you a number because it gets a little weird, we moved into our home in May. We have three bathrooms, and we didn't have to buy toilet paper until the end of December.

It took about two months before everything was sorted and put away. We donated so much stuff that whenever we drove by Goodwill I expected the staff would run out and applaud.

I thought he was on the packrat wagon but, sadly, he relapsed. He went to the store for a bottle of wine and a birthday card. He came home with the wine, the card and <u>10 gallons</u> of fruit punch…because it was ON SALE!

A couple of important facts: First, neither of us drinks fruit punch. Second, while it's true our granddaughters visit on occasion, none of them are camels!

I didn't want to do it but I had to institute a moratorium: until further notice, he is no longer allowed in a store without me. Unless it's a jewelry store, of course. I'm not cruel.

So, I have to deal with Jeff's packrat-edness. However, he has his own struggles with me. My life is a series of embarrassing moments and he's often caught in the fray.

My first "moment" after Jeff and I were in our new home happened two days after we moved. He left very early in the morning for work and I started going through a box of my accessories to put things away. The TV installer was due in about 30 minutes, which gave me plenty of time to finish the box and get dressed as I was still in my jammies. Wouldn't you know, right that second the doorbell rang. The TV guy was early!

At first I didn't know what to do but decided my pajamas were sort of like loungewear and it's ok to wear loungewear around the house, so I answered the door.

The young man gave me kind of a strange look, which I attributed to my outfit, but was otherwise friendly and professional. He began his work and I returned to unpacking. When he was done, I escorted him to the front porch, thanked him for everything and waved goodbye, also taking the opportunity to wave to a few of our new neighbors who happened to be outside.

Back in the house, I walked by a mirror only then realizing I was still in my pajamas, err, loungewear. Worse, I was also wearing a tiara I had found in the box of accessories. I had absentmindedly stuck it on my head and promptly forgot about it. *This* was the ensemble I shared with the TV man and my new neighbors.

I told Jeff about it. Since they were *our* neighbors, it was really *our* first embarrassing moment. It was also his first facepalm about me. Ah, love.

Elizabeth A. Winter-Sharpe

The Mothball Incident

A few months before Jeff and I got married, my niece and I made centerpieces and prepared various other items for the wedding. Jeff kindly produced some empty tote boxes and packed everything away for me until the big day arrived.

A week before our wedding, I opened the boxes for a final check and was overwhelmed by the smell of MOTHBALLS! Evidently, mothballs had been stored in the totes before and now everything reeked!

I was nearly hysterical. Jeff was unconcerned. "What's wrong with a little mothball smell? No one will notice."

I called my daughter-in-law-to-be, who was making the cake – the only thing at the wedding that wouldn't smell like mothballs - and poured my heart out. She was ready to mobilize help but neither of us knew what to do. (Upon hearing what happened, the oldest granddaughter noted with a laugh, "That's Grandpa!" Apparently, Jeff had a reputation of which I was unaware.)

I turned to the Internet and learned mothball is second only to skunk as the most difficult odor to remove, I began buying deodorizers of all types and purchased copious amounts of cinnamon oil to overwhelm, hopefully replace, the odor.

Always positive, Jeff would smell the offending items every day and tell me, "I can't smell a thing, dear. Problem solved!" Of course, I could smell it from across the room and told him, "You're just saying that because you don't want me to cry again."

Two days before our wedding, Jeff called me at work to tell me that the odor was gone. He said he knew I'd be skeptical so he had taken a box of wedding supplies door to door in our neighborhood for "independent smell tests" and everything passed.

To this day, I have no idea if our wedding smelled like mothballs or not but, if it did, I offer my heartfelt thanks to our guests for being too polite to tell me.

Elizabeth A. Winter-Sharpe

On the Rocks

My first marriage was over long before I filed for divorce.

Staying way past closing is part of my M.O. - my marriage, my job, some friendships. I get stuck in a cycle of being ready to move on and then I think about the good times, the good qualities, the successes. I resolve to find those things again, not willing to admit that they have long since died or never existed in the first place, other than in my mind.

Of course, regarding my marriage, there was also the fact that I took a vow. One I believed with all my heart and soul. A vow. My word. My honor. How could I end a marriage when I promised to love, honor and cherish him until one of us died? Or, as I began to ask God, how soon can one of us die?

I suggested marriage counseling and, to my surprise, he agreed. "Anything if it will fix you," he said, succinctly demonstrating his utter belief that if I were only a better person, not to mention thin, we wouldn't have any problems.

About six weeks in, the marriage counselor pulled me aside and said, "You need to get a divorce. Now. The sooner the better."

Surprised, I mentioned that she didn't seem to be following the standard operating procedure for marriage counselors, e.g. "Aren't you supposed to be helping us save our marriage?"

"He is abusive. He abuses you in front of me, what he tells me happens at home is abuse. I can only imagine how bad it is when there are no witnesses."

Tales of the Terminally Awkward

I was embarrassed and ashamed. I knew better than this. I've advised others about how they're treated by their loved ones. But I took a vow.

I tried to be a better person, practically turning myself inside out, always questioning my actions, always second-guessing myself until I was barely able to make a decision. His other complaint to the marriage counselor was I lacked self-confidence. He didn't see the irony.

In the midst of all this, my company reorganized and I was let go from my job; a job I had held for 25 years, building a department from the ground up. Still, it wasn't the worst thing that happened that day. The worst thing happened when I got home.

I told my husband and he said, "I'm sorry this happened to you but you'd better figure it out and get another job or as many jobs as it takes to keep us in this lifestyle. I am not going back to work. This is all on you."

His remark was a slap in the face. I wasn't his partner; I was his benefactor.

I was up all night thinking about my life, my work and my marriage. I finally faced the fact that I was in the relationship because I thought I didn't deserve any better, because fixing his problems is what made me feel worthwhile and loveable. The next day I told my husband I wanted a divorce and we separated. I made a conscious decision to take charge of my life and my happiness.

I had always lived by the "never let them see you sweat" philosophy, which was pretty far from my reality. But I got a job, I got a divorce and I got a drill.

I felt owning a drill somehow meant I could take care of my house, which I quickly learned was untrue. The first time I ever used the drill, I took down some shelves and ended up with more holes in the wall than when I started. But, dammit, the shelves came down!

The year after my divorce was fraught with failure and I mostly learned to ask for help and find people I could trust. I

Elizabeth A. Winter-Sharpe

had to hire people, negotiate deals, and fire people, which is difficult if you're worried about people liking you.

The biggest challenge of all was when I decided I wanted to start dating again. I had some work to do because I would *not* repeat my marriage.

I realized all my romantic relationships were based on me being a rescuer – trying to make him happy by solving his problems, including those he created himself, all while rationalizing his bad behavior.

I also realized I would always "go along to get along," focusing only on my partner's needs and wants, at the expense of my own, with everything from choosing a restaurant to buying a house.

Finally, I realized if I wanted to be happy, I had to commit to being the real me, being open and honest about who I am, what I like and don't like, my fears and my flaws. I had to risk rejection because a potential partner might not like the "real" me. In that case, I had to accept he's not the right partner for me.

Most important, I realized I could be happy on my own. I *wanted* a relationship but I didn't *need* one.

Once I committed to being me, I had to figure out "him". As most decisions in my life, this one started with a list. It included all of the qualities I wanted in a partner. One might expect many of these qualities to be a given but, I wasn't taking any chances.

The list, in alphabetical order, was:
- Ethical
- Fun, enjoys life, likes to travel
- Great sense of humor, loves to laugh
- Hard-worker, ideally a professional
- Honest
- Kind
- Loving, affectionate
- Loving, happy, tight-knit family
- Mature

- Partner, understands marriage secrets and signals
- Similar values
- Smart, ideally a college graduate
- Thoughtful
- Trustworthy
- Bonus item: tall

Armed with my list, I started dating. I dubbed myself the "one and done" dater because, throughout the conversation, I mentally went through the checklist and more often than not, I declined a second date.

I must emphasize that not fulfilling the items on my list was not necessarily a shortcoming on the man's part. For example, I love to travel. I went out with a man who hated to travel. He was a good person but we were a bad match.

The greatest lesson for me was that choosing to be alone, choosing my well-being, choosing the right person for me or choosing to stay single, was empowering.

Then a man asked me for two first dates.

I was trying online dating and heard from a man named Jeff. We exchanged a few messages and had many similar interests. Then I received this message: "I'd like to take you out for coffee and the next day for dinner. Yes, Beth, I'm asking you for two first dates."

The old me would have said "yes" immediately even though I had serious reservations. I wouldn't want to make someone feel bad even if I was uncomfortable. Instead, I responded I'd be more comfortable planning just one date. He agreed.

When we met, I first noticed he had kind eyes. He was also very considerate and had impeccable manners. At 6'8", he more than met my bonus item. Curiously, I felt at home with him, like we "fit."

Our conversation was easy, interesting and fun. Then he told me loves to dance and I thought, "Here we go."

I took a deep breath and announced, "Well, just so you know, I'm clumsy and I can't dance well!" Then I braced myself.

I don't know what went through his mind but he just looked at me, shrugged and said "okay" and went on with the conversation.

Whether his reaction empowered me or created a monster, over the next few weeks I was full of announcements of what I like and what I don't like, my fears and flaws. Jeff sometimes asked more about it but that was it.

Once after a random pronouncement I said, "I know you wish I was different. Why don't you just say it?" He looked at me with those kind eyes and said, "God made you exactly how he wants you and I don't question his work. I like you exactly how you are." Wow.

Sixteen months after we met, Jeff and I were married. We laugh every day. We find joy every day. I have a wonderful, extended family that has embraced me.

We have faced hardships as partners. Just two weeks after we were married, I lost my job. When I told Jeff, he hugged me and said, "We'll be fine. We have each other and we'll figure it out together." A month later, when he lost his job, I said the same to him.

Moonlight and roses aside, it's still a marriage. Sometimes, he annoys me. Occasionally, he makes me mad. (Yes, I'm sure Jeff could say the same about me.) I was puzzled. He met all fourteen of my requirements, plus the bonus item. How could he annoy me?

I realized that I had become a little fuzzy on the 14 qualities that were oh so important to me back in the day but I could easily list the things that bothered me. That struck me as wrong and I decided to intentionally focus on the positive.

I bought a big glass jar and a stack of blank business cards. Starting on our wedding anniversary, every day for an entire year I wrote down one thing I loved about him.

It didn't matter if I was annoyed or sick or we had a boring day. All that mattered was that I could think of some reason I loved him **that day**. Maybe he did laundry, or bought me flowers or winked at me at a party. Maybe it was the way his eyes soften when he smiles at me or the day I called him with great news (I had been asked to speak at a national conference) and he guessed my great news was that I was going to make spaghetti and meatballs for dinner. Or maybe because I was not being my best self and he hugged me anyway.

On our next wedding anniversary, I gave the jar to Jeff. To be sure, it was NOT a hallmark moment. When Jeff doesn't know what to say, he simply says, "Wow." He said "wow" three times. When I explained to him what I did and why I did it, he said, "I annoy you?"

The next morning, his first words were, "I can't get over how thoughtful you are. You gave me such a wonderful gift." What he didn't realize is the extent of the gift.

Now, I focus on the positive rather than the negative. I am grateful for the good things, rather than resigned to the "bad."

I have 106 drill bits and at least 365 reasons for loving Jeff. Well, 366 – he still doesn't care that I can't dance well.

Elizabeth A. Winter-Sharpe

So Long, Farewell

The Sound of Music is my all-time favorite movie. Say what you will but it just makes me happy.

Jeff has watched it with me a couple of times and didn't bat an eye when I sang every part of every song. He drew the line at trying to dance the Laendler, or playing Georg to my Maria. Instead, he did me one better.

A year and a half after our wedding, we took our honeymoon to Europe, visiting Germany, Austria, and Switzerland. While in Austria, we went to Mondsee and renewed our vows at the Basilika St. Michael, the wedding church from the movie. It was wonderful and romantic.

Though decidedly different types of memories, I hope you enjoyed reading the essays in this book. Like our vow renewal, these are a few of my favorite things.

☺

About the Author

Elizabeth and her husband, Jeff, live in Northeast Ohio with their two cats, Raleigh and Radley.

Made in the USA
Monee, IL
12 December 2021